Improvising Careers

PRAISE FOR *IMPROVISING CAREERS*

Chris Bishop deconstructs the myth of the linear career path and rebuilds it for our dynamic age. This smart and timely book offers both a practical framework and a broader mindset for staying relevant in an era of automation and rapid change.
    Daniel H. Pink, #1 *New York Times* best-selling author of *THE POWER OF REGRET* and *DRIVE*

Christopher Bishop's book, *Improvising Careers: Succeed at Jobs that Don't Exist Yet,* contains a powerful message with hands-on tools to help readers prepare for the workplace of the future!
    Dorie Clark, *Wall Street Journal* best-selling author of *The Long Game* and executive education faculty, Columbia Business School

Whether you are just starting college or in mid-career or getting ready to retire and explore new adventures, Bishop's book, *Improvising Careers,* provides exciting and practical guidance on how to make your next successful career move . . . and the one(s) after that!
    Jonathan Fanton, president Emeritus at the American Academy of Arts and Sciences

Improvising Careers: Succeed at Jobs that Don't Exist Yet empowers readers for continuous lifelong learning, upskilling, and reskilling as civilization faces difficult challenges. The author provides pragmatic insights and tools to make moving from career to career a natural part of a life design process. *Improvising Careers* also provides tools to enable readers to be successful in the era of the gig economy and the global borderless workplace.

Chris Dede, senior research fellow, Harvard Graduate School of Education; associate director for Research, National AI Institute for Adult Learning and Online Education; author of *Learning Engineering for Online Education*

Bishop has had eight different careers so far, including touring rock musician and fifteen years at IBM, as well as working in the jingle business in New York City. His own personal path led him to investigate how jobs and skill needs have changed over the centuries, and he developed his Future Career Toolkit to help today's learners be successful in the twenty-first century's global borderless workplace—no matter what career(s) they pursue.

Ben Pring, leading speaker; co-author of the best-selling book *What to Do When Machines Do Everything;* advisor on the Future of Work and the Intersection of Cutting Edge Technology and Business

Christopher Bishop has done us all a tremendous favor by writing this book. In my Creativity workshops, we acknowledge we are all facing a Future of Unknowable Unknowns: constant unpredictable changes; more fierce disruptions like the one we just went through but the next won't be anything like the one we just went through; and unimaginable technology breakthroughs that will generate

waves of wonderful opportunities. So, how do we prepare for an Unknowable Future? Read Christopher's book. It is engaging and will provide you with the tools and perspectives you need.
Carl Nordgren, entrepreneur; creativity consultant; novelist; radio host; author of *Becoming a Creative Genius (again); former adjunct professor, Duke University*

A career is no longer a linear path but a dynamic journey of adaptation and reinvention. *Improvising Careers* shows you how to embrace this reality and thrive in the twenty-first-century workplace.
David Blake, founder and co-CEO, Degreed

In a world where careers are becoming increasingly fluid and unpredictable, Christopher Bishop's *Improvising Careers: Succeed at Jobs That Don't Exist Yet* offers a refreshing and practical approach. His Future Career Toolkit provides essential guidance for navigating the ever-evolving landscape of work and provides readers with actionable tools and insights to thrive in the future workplace, no matter how unconventional their career path may be.
Jennifer McClure, CEO of Unbridled Talent and Chief Excitement Officer of DisruptHR

Improvising Careers is more than a book; it's a blueprint for lifelong career adaptability. Bishop's pragmatic insights and tools make transitioning between careers feel natural and purposeful, especially in today's gig economy and global workplace. The title alone hooks you, and the content delivers on its promise, addressing the impact of emerging technologies like GenAI and quantum information science.

Lolly Daskal, executive leadership coach; author of *The Leadership Gap: What Gets Between You and Your Greatness*

Whether you're seeking a career in whatever technology comes after GenAI, medical 3D printing, brain-computer interfaces, quantum algorithm development, or autonomous drone choreography, Bishop lays out techniques for identifying the organizations leading the charge and how to acquire the skills needed to get hired by them!

Nathalie Nahai, keynote speaker; consultant; author of *Business Unusual;* host of Nathalie Nahai in Conversation

Like great comedy and jazz, today's careers reward skilled improvisation. Christopher Bishop channels his own "nonlinear, multimodal" career riffs into lessons for next-generation careers—always listening, learning, and ready to pivot. His own career has morphed from performer to technologist, educator, and now author. University students, career counselors, mentors, and CHROs can all benefit from these optimistic insights.

Roger Mader, managing partner, Ampersand; chief customer officer, Myra; author, *Purposeful Enterprise*

Improvising Careers delivers sharp, practical advice for everyone—from college students to mid-career workers to top executives. It's a guide for those eager to redefine their roles in today's limitless, global workplace.

Laurie Ruettimann, Keynote Speaker; podcaster; author, *Punk Rock HR*

As technology in the workplace evolves at lightning speed, Christopher Bishop's *Improvising Careers* is a must-read guide for navigating uncharted career paths. With practical insights and a forward-thinking approach, Bishop arms readers with the essential toolkit to not just survive—but thrive—in roles that haven't even been invented yet. A fantastic resource for anyone ready to take charge of their future in our all too uncertain world of work.

Gina London, Emmy-winning former network journalist and CEO, Language of Leadership, Ltd.

Careers and skill needs have been shifting for centuries, if not thousands of years. Bishop's book *Improvising Careers* provides a Future Career Toolkit to help readers find their place in this constantly evolving career landscape!

Oliver Sidwell, co-presenter, The Jack & Ollie Show | The Early Careers Podcast

Christopher Bishop's *Improvising Careers* offers a pioneering roadmap for navigating the ever-shifting world of work. Focusing on jobs that don't even exist yet, the book presents a bold yet grounded exploration of the future workforce, blending humanity, science, and foresight in a way that feels both visionary and achievable.

> **Perry Timms**, founder and chief energy officer,
> People & Transformational HR, Ltd.

Improvising Careers is a masterclass in adaptability and continuous learning—the two most critical skills for thriving in today's AI and data-driven economy. Bishop's personal journey and practical tools offer an inspiring and actionable blueprint for reskilling at scale.

> **David Yakobovitch**, general partner at
> DataPower Ventures

Christopher Bishop's *Improvising Careers* is an essential read for anyone navigating the ever-changing landscape of the modern workforce. His insights, honed from a remarkable career that spans eight distinct professions, provide a blueprint for thriving in jobs that don't even exist yet. This book not only offers a fascinating historical perspective on how work has evolved but also equips readers with actionable tools through the Future Career Toolkit to succeed in the twenty-first century's global, borderless workplace. Whether you're just starting out, mid-career, or considering your next chapter, *Improvising Careers* will inspire and guide you every step of the way.

> **Dr. Kiko Suarez**, leadership coach and
> education executive

The times they are a-changin'—and today's workers are part of a continuum of careers and skill needs that have been shifting for centuries. Bishop's book *Improvising Careers* provides not only a fascinating historical perspective but also a Future Career Toolkit to help readers shift to their next career . . . and the ones after that!

Dennis F. Bonilla, talent & leadership alchemist/mentor/coach; lifelong learning evangelist; digital learning & technology transformation strategist

Bishop's journey from touring musician to IBM strategist to quantum tech evangelist isn't just fascinating—it's a masterclass in career adaptation. His Future Career Toolkit, born from decades of successful reinvention, offers practical guidance for anyone looking to thrive in our rapidly evolving workplace. This isn't just theory—it's hard-won wisdom from someone who's repeatedly transformed his career path.

Paul Estes, editor-in-chief, Enterprise AI Today; best-selling author, *Gig Mindset*

It was a lot of fun working with Chris Bishop to invent his Future Career Toolkit. We took the various ideation processes I've developed to solve tough corporate challenges for the past twenty-five years and modified them to address various career reinvention opportunities. This led to truly original approaches and techniques—that really work—to help people reimagine their next career . . . and the one(s) after that!"

Bryan Mattimore, cofounder and chief idea guy, Growth Engine Innovation Agency; Author, *21 Days to a Big Idea*

IMPROVISING CAREERS

Succeed at Jobs That Don't Exist Yet

Christopher Bishop

NEW YORK

LONDON • NASHVILLE • MELBOURNE • VANCOUVER

Improvising Careers

Succeed At Jobs That Don't Exist Yet

© 2025 Christopher Bishop

All rights reserved. No portion of this book may be reproduced, stored in a retrieval system, or transmitted in any form or by any means—electronic, mechanical, photocopy, recording, scanning, or other—except for brief quotations in critical reviews or articles, without the prior written permission of the publisher.

Published in New York, New York, by Morgan James Publishing. Morgan James is a trademark of Morgan James, LLC. www.MorganJamesPublishing.com

Proudly distributed by Publishers Group West®

ISBN 9781636985589 paperback
ISBN 9781636985596 ebook
Library of Congress Control Number: 2024943497

Cover Design by:
Ale Urquide

Interior Design by:
Chris Treccani
www.3dogcreative.net

Morgan James is a proud partner of Habitat for Humanity Peninsula and Greater Williamsburg. Partners in building since 2006.

Get involved today! Visit: www.morgan-james-publishing.com/giving-back

To Lee and Cole

CONTENTS

Acknowledgments — *xvii*
Introduction — *xix*

Chapter 1	Why This Book?	1
Chapter 2	Rethinking Work in Modern Times	9
Chapter 3	Carving Spears to Writing Algorithms	23
Chapter 4	Brace Yourself for a Future of Solar Sails and Ingestible Robots	33
Chapter 5	Getting Down to Busine$$	41
Chapter 6	Connect the Dots	51
Chapter 7	Think Like a Genius	63
Chapter 8	Overview of the Future Toolkit	73
Chapter 9	Where Do You Stand Out? "VOICE"	79
Chapter 10	Fine-Tuning Your Info-Gathering "ANTENNA"	91
Chapter 11	"MESH" With the Right People	121
Chapter 12	Taking the Long View	139
Afterword	My Story	145

Images from the Journey — *179*
About the Author — *185*
Endnotes — *189*

ACKNOWLEDGMENTS

I want to thank my editor, Randy Peyser, for her patient, intentional, and methodical approach, which kept me focused and consistently working toward the goal of writing a book. I also want to thank Sarah Adams for her brilliant wordsmithing and finessing, which turned my sometimes rambling language into intelligible and engaging prose.

Thanks also to my publisher, David Hancock, for believing in me and providing the opportunity to bring this book to the world; to the team at Morgan James—Bethany Marshall, Gayle West, Christopher Kirk, and Krissy Nelson—for their patience in guiding me through the myriad stages of the publishing process.

Most of all, I am forever grateful to my beautiful, patient wife, Lee, for her unwavering love and support throughout my atypical career journey.

INTRODUCTION

I often try to imagine going back in time to have a conversation with my Scottish grandmother about what people are doing to make a living in the twenty-first century.

Calista Caldow was born in 1896 in Saratoga Springs, New York, at a time when most people still lit their homes with gaslights and candles. In fact, it would be another fifty years before electricity was widely installed in people's homes. As I picture the world she grew up in, I fantasize about telling her that I would someday have a job running a team of people who produced locations on the "World Wide Web" where large companies could sell their products with just the click of a button. I try to imagine the look on her face when I tell her that my job after that was promoting computers based on the principles of quantum mechanics.

I try to picture her reaction to the news that a great-grandson of hers would have a job putting panels on the roofs of houses that convert sunshine into electricity. Or that another great-grandson would be working in "techno agriculture," running an indoor medical marijuana farm in his home. Or that yet another great-grandson would be employed by a company that makes cars that can actually drive themselves. I imagine her jaw dropping and her eyes getting wide.

"The World Wide what?!" she'd say. "What kinds of jobs are those?"

Then I would tell her that I authored a book about the future of work, not using a No. 2 pencil and a legal pad but by speaking into a piece of glass and steel that I could hold in my hand as it turned what I said into electronic text. Needless to say, she would shake her head and think it was all just science fiction.

And yet, you, dear reader, will have equally mind-blowing conversations with your grandchildren. The jobs that do not exist yet are being created even as you read these words. And those future careers will seem like magical, sci-fi endeavors to those of us sitting here in the early decades of the twenty-first century.

My Journey So Far

I often describe myself as a "nonlinear, multimodal careerist." I proudly wear this title based on the eight careers I have navigated since graduating from college in 1972. I have worked as a rock musician all over the world, as a commercial jingle producer in New York City, and as a website project manager for some of the first corporate websites in the mid-1990s.

In fact, the very reason I wrote this book is to share how I successfully navigated various and seemingly unrelated careers . . . all to help you prepare for the rapidly emerging global borderless workplace on the horizon.

I have reflected extensively on the reasons, motivations, and processes that led me to transition from career to career. I hope these reflections guide anyone looking to make a career move, explore new opportunities, and apply their skills and experience to new business models in the increasingly global work world.

"When I Was Your Age..."

I used to wince when people older than me used *that* phrase, yet here I am. But to give you some perspective on my journey: when I graduated from college in the 1970s, there were no smartphones, no personal computers, no electric cars, or social media. Believe it or not, I used to listen to music on LPs (those black vinyl discs that are now making a bit of a comeback as "vintage"). CDs had not been invented yet, and I still wrote actual letters home to my family while I was in college. In fact, when I went to England in 1973 with a band to record my first album, my parents actually sent me a telegram congratulating me on my success!

Compared to how I grew up, being able to download a book to your phone or tablet in thirty seconds and start absorbing the content right away is revolutionary. Just a few years ago, being able to move funds between accounts and pay bills on your smartphone while riding in a self-driving vehicle would have been viewed as completely ridiculous.

The changes I have seen in just five decades of living make my head spin. We are just in the initial stages of this era. Historians will no doubt look back on this as the "pre-history" of technology's impact on society, culture, and, more specifically, jobs and careers.

THREE EPIPHANIES

Three transformational tipping points inspired me to write this book. I want to share a bit of detail about them with you for context.

Epiphany #1 Music as Data

My first epiphany for how jobs and careers were evolving took place when I was living in New York City. For several years I had been able to make a living as a freelance bass player, ready to play music in whatever style paid some cash. But then a transformation took place, starting slowly and then ultimately taking over. Technology advances allowed music to become data on computers, rather than sound emitted from real, live instruments. Back then, I decided to jump in and learn how to compose music on a computer to stay viable and make a living. But more on that later.

Epiphany #2 Enterprise of the Future

A second event tied to my understanding of how work evolves occurred when I was working as a strategy consultant at IBM around 2001. I was invited to join the Enterprise of the Future consortium, an initiative led by a Distinguished Engineer from IBM Research. He created a team to develop scenarios for what corporate business models might look like in the next five to ten years. The people on the team were all brilliant technical minds, many from the IBM Academy of Technology. One of my roles on the team was to bring real-world business challenges to the conversations. I found the sessions fascinating and felt very lucky to be invited to participate. It was my first introduction to a bigger perspective on conversations about business models being tied to technology, how the models had changed over time, and how experts theorized about how things would evolve next.

Epiphany #3 College Keynote Address

The third and final trigger that drove my interest in the future workplace was a request from my alma mater, Bennington College, in 2006. The alumni relations person invited me to deliver a keynote address about what I had been doing since graduating, my story of having navigated through various careers, and how that tied to Bennington's focus on designing your own education.

This invitation itself got me thinking more broadly, not only about how I had come to navigate these various careers but also about how my path was part of a larger pattern of historical transformations driven by changes in business models, technology, and culture. The rate and pace at which careers and skills are changing today made my own perspective even more compelling.

It suddenly dawned on me that I had experienced how today's learners will live and work in the twenty-first century's global borderless economy. I had actually lived this evolving model! So, I began to try to codify how I did it and what lessons I learned. As a result, I put together a presentation and workshop that would help learners be successful on their multi-career journeys.

Outcomes of My Multi-Career Navigation

Since that first speech at Bennington, I have continued to hone a workshop entitled "How to Succeed at Jobs that Don't Exist Yet." I've conducted these workshops all over the US, including at Columbia, Duke, Queens College, NYU, Texas A&M, and Union College. I have also given talks at the London School of Economics, London Business School, King's College London, Royal Holloway University, the Institute of Physics and the National Physical Laboratory in the UK.

I've talked with groups ranging from seventh-grade Career Day students to senior executives at various outplacement firms. In January 2020, I completed an online video course for LinkedIn Learning called "Future-proofing your data science career" providing guidance for success in that specific discipline. I try to give audiences in my workshops practical advice on how to do something to that generates income and also helps them feel more fulfilled.

Burnished in the Crucible

As you'll see, over the years, I've mapped my own nonlinear journey, like the shifts in my own personal desires and which objectives warranted self-reflection. I've also investigated my interests to find a match for my skills at a macro level. It is a process that has taken place over and over again in my own career journey. And as I began to analyze and reflect on my multiple careers, certain insights around patterns and processes began to emerge. Increased awareness of my own shifting goals and objectives always led me to make changes in my personal direction. Whether I was moving from being a touring bass player with various bands to a role producing commercial jingles or being a Web producer or designing executive communications in a corporate setting, it was always a range of factors that motivated me to move into a new role.

So, in writing this book, I didn't spend hours in a library archive reading papers with endless citations of other papers to come to these conclusions and develop this approach. These concepts were burnished in the crucible of real life, schlepping around New York City in the wind and rain trying to get someone to hire me so I could pay the rent and the electric bill. Each time I embarked on a new career, I learned new skills to carry into the next job.

Why It Matters Now

The fact is that the rate and pace at which business and global economies are morphing and being disrupted will require people to have expertise in many new skills, often called twenty-first century skills.

More and more college graduates today are unable to find work based on what they have learned in school. This book is designed to provide guidance not only as to what to study but also how to manage finding the right opportunity in today's morphing workplace.

Here are a few salient points to keep in mind about the status of the current workplace. Perhaps you, dear reader, can relate to some of them:

As of September 2023, Gen Z makes up 17.1 million workers in the US full-time workforce. This is 11.6 percent of the US workforce and 37 percent of the global workforce.

As of January 2023, fifty-six million millennials were in the US workforce, which is 35 percent of the total labor force.

More than half of US workers—61 percent—are considering leaving their jobs in 2023, a new report from LinkedIn has found, noting that a higher percentage of Gen Z (defined by LinkedIn as ages eighteen to twenty-five) and millennial (ages twenty-six to forty-one) workers are planning to call it quits than any other generation.[1]

A recent Gallup report on the millennial generation reveals that 21 percent of millennials say they've changed jobs within the past year, more than three times the number of non-millennials who report the same.

This report found that 60 percent of millennials say they are open to a different job opportunity—fifteen percentage points higher than the percentage of non-millennial workers who say the same.

millennials are also the most willing to act on better opportunities: 36 percent report that they will look for a job with a different organization in the next twelve months if the job market improves, compared with 21 percent of non-millennials who say the same.

Because successful companies need to develop so rapidly, they will be looking for workers who can connect unlikely dots to help them create products and services that address new and emerging market opportunities. What does this mean for you? Rather than focusing on a single area of expertise to compete in the global workplace, you must be a creative problem solver. You'll need to be comfortable with ambiguity, be resourceful and resilient, and be able to work across disciplines. You'll need to be able to figure out what you need to learn, learn it, apply it, and then do it all over again. You'll need to be aware of your role as a global citizen, and you'll need these skills regardless of age, geographic location, or level of technology skills. They will be essential for navigating the new workplace.

I have tried to develop these ideas for learners of any age who are thinking about what to study, how and what to learn, and which career move to make next. The concepts in this book certainly apply to anyone who is interested in making a shift or who wants to find a way to completely change direction to do something more fulfilling, more comfortable, and more soul-satisfying—whatever your motivations are. Only you know.

My general advice regarding career paths is to chase the maelstrom, find the chaos, go for the mayhem. Go where they don't know what "it" is yet, in this case, "it" being existing, traditional business models. Then you can help shape "it," help design and develop "it," and not only have a vested interest in its success but also have an opportunity to be a leader in an evolving space. (The Future Career Toolkit is designed to help you identify where the maelstrom is taking place.)

WHAT TO EXPECT ...

Here is an overview of how the book is organized to help you find the content you are most interested in.

Chapter 1: Why This Book?
I start by discussing the meta-factors driving the transformation to a global borderless workplace in the twenty-first century and how and why technologies are transforming business models.

Chapter 2: Rethinking Work in Modern Times
This chapter is an examination of the major shift in the way employers and employees interact with one another and an exploration of how pandemic-driven trends like The Great Resignation and Quiet Quitting are actually expressions of broader trends around how people view work.

Chapter 3: Carving Spears to Quantum Algorithms: How the World Has Evolved Over the Centuries
The best way to understand forward-thinking topics is to understand how the past has molded today's workplace. In this chapter, I examine the various ways that unconnected disciplines have been at the heart of new career creation in the past.

Chapter 4: Brace Yourself for a Future of Solar Sails and Ingestible Robots: It's Always About Technology
Technology continues to drive breathtaking upheaval in every aspect of civilization and society. In this section, I share

my perspective on how every discipline is being transformed and the implications for jobs, skills, and careers.

Chapter 5: Getting Down to Busine$$

Today's job creation and career evolution processes are based on market-driven global economics. Innovative companies early in the twenty-first century based their hiring on very different models than those that existed in the past. To stay viable and employable, today's workers must remember that careers are part of a larger mechanism of job creation and destruction driven by the desire to improve business outcomes.

Chapter 6: Connect the Dots: The Intersection of Unlikely Disciplines

Careers, driven by economic factors, have evolved at the intersection of the old and the new. In this chapter, I examine how business models appear, morph, and then disappear, leveraging existing technologies or combining them with new approaches. No one lights their dining room with whale oil anymore.

Chapter 7: Think Like a Genius: Lessons for the Next Generation of Polymaths

I believe that everyone has the potential to "think like a genius" based on their own skills and proclivities. Learning more about this mindset will help you be successful in the new global marketplace, so I'm sharing some insights on historical figures who have navigated multiple careers.

Chapters 8-11: Future Career Toolkit

The core of this book focuses on my Future Career Toolkit—VOICE, ANTENNA, and MESH—and how to understand and apply these three tools. I developed them based on my career journey of fifty years in the workplace.

I have dedicated a chapter to each of the three tools and an intro to orient you to the overall concepts in each one. My objective is to give you real-world tools to help you identify your own strengths and passions, provide guidance on tapping into the channels where forward-looking conversations on these topics are happening, and then teach you how to track down and connect with the people and organizations who are leading those conversations.

Chapter 12: Taking the Long View

I end the book with final comments on how to stay alert in your journey and how to learn, unlearn, and relearn when moving through different careers. I also encourage those seeking new career paths.

Afterword: My Story—Navigating Eight Different Careers with a Degree in German Lit

This chapter contains more personal stories and insights about my nonlinear careers. I have included it to give you tangible examples of the various challenges I faced and the decisions I made to address them. I have also called out "teachable moments" tied to various transitions.

Images from the Journey: pictures from my various careers

We are at a seminal moment in the history of careers and work. There are lots of opportunities to do really exciting things! My goal for this book is to help you hone your focus on what you can do now to ensure a successful series of careers, as well as how to future-proof your skills on a macro level. Hopefully, the content in the following chapters will get you excited about exploring the many new options available to you on your own nonlinear, multimodal career path. I look forward to hearing about all the great stuff you are doing. So read on, and let's get started!

– CHAPTER 1 –

Why This Book?

Nanopharmacist? Lunar tour guide? Robotic ethics consultant? Augmented reality content designer? Quantum algorithm developer? Bioprinting software manager? Neuralink implant fabricator? These jobs may not sound too familiar, but they will in due time.

The world of work is being transformed!

A ONCE-IN-A-LIFETIME CHANGE

According to the World Economic Forum's "The Future of Jobs 2020," over the next ten years, more than one billion workers are at risk of losing their jobs to robotics, automation, and AI. They estimate that by "2025, 85 million jobs may be displaced by a shift in the division of labor between humans and machines, while ninety-seven million new roles may emerge that are more adapted to the new division of labor between humans, machines and algorithms."

Consultancy firm Oxford Economics released a study on robotics and industrial automation in 2019 that suggested a loss of twenty million jobs by 2030, a number that represents nearly half of all jobs in industrialized countries.

Think about this quote from organizational consultant and author, Warren Bennis. "The factory of the future will have only two employees, a man and a dog. The man will be there to feed the dog. The dog will be there to keep the man from touching the equipment."

A recent report from the MIT Work of the Future Task Force states that "spectacular advances in computing and communications, robotics, AI, and manufacturing processes are reshaping industries as diverse as insurance, retail, healthcare, manufacturing, and logistics and transportation."

Steven Rattner, who served as lead adviser to the Presidential Task Force on the Auto Industry in 2009, wisely stated in his *New York Times* op-ed, "Fear Not the Coming of the Robots," "The trick is not to protect old jobs, as the Luddites who endeavored to smash all machinery sought to do, but to create new ones. And since the invention of the wheel, that's what has occurred."

Meeting Market Demand

To explore the tremendous opportunities that lie ahead for today's learners in the workplace of the future, *Improvising Careers* provides readers with tools to shape and take advantage of the coming technological innovations.

Peter Diamondis, founder and executive chairman of the XPRIZE Foundation and executive founder of Singularity

University, recently released his report on twenty Metatrends for the 2020s. The report describes transformational technologies such as augmented human longevity, the smart economy, AI-human collaboration, urbanized cellular agriculture, and high-bandwidth brain-computer interfaces . . . to name just a few. The implications for future careers are clear.

From a meta-level, global gigabit satellite-enabled connectivity will provide low-cost ubiquitous communications for everyone, everywhere. It will transform the concept of what work is and how and wherever it gets done, whether it is on Earth, on the Moon, on Mars, in a space station or on an asteroid.

You will work in a global borderless workplace in an era of increasingly interconnected global business models. Get ready to collaborate with people who are located in many different physical locations and come from varying ethnic and cultural backgrounds.

While some may be apprehensive about the kinds of workplace transformations underway, history and economics show no inherent conflict between technological change, full employment, and increased wages—quite the contrary. Innovation has historically improved the overall quality of workers' lives while always creating occupations that require new kinds of expertise, as well as opportunities for rewarding work.

The effect of technologies like AI, machine learning, and robotics on the labor market is visible across every vertical and discipline. The time is now to prepare the future workforce to understand and embrace these trends. As innovative technologies are increasingly embedded deeply into businesses, government agencies, and other organizations, it is clear that many of the current workplace models, their attendant skill needs, and the careers they represent are often decades-old artifacts. Some are even from the last century.

Needless to say, the impact of bleeding-edge technologies like cryptoassets, CRISPR, blockchain, nanotechnology, and quantum information science will not just affect workers' career choices but will also dictate regulatory and policy guidelines while driving broader cultural changes.

Living Longer Means Working Longer

Another crucial driver of workplace transformation is longevity. Since the middle of the last century, general life expectancy has been increasing by one year every five years. Living a longer life means being in the workplace longer. According to a May 2017 report by the World Economic Forum, someone born in 1947 might have had an average life expectancy of eighty-five, but about half of the babies born in the US in 2007 are predicted to live to 104, compared with the United Kingdom, where life expectancy is 103, and Japan, where life expectancy is 107.

In her book, *100 Plus: How the Coming Age of Longevity Will Change Everything, From Careers and Relationships to Family and Faith*, author Sonia Arrison speculates that some babies born today may live to be 150 years old.

People will need to start preparing for the kinds of work they might be doing as they move into their eighties, nineties, and beyond. My "Future Career Toolkit" enables readers to better plan and execute their own nonlinear, multimodal career path. The tools consist of three main components that are defined and expanded upon in individual chapters: VOICE, ANTENNA, and MESH. These tools provide a systematized, scalable, repeatable, malleable framework for navigating multiple careers, both today and in the future.

New Business Models Drive Career Options

Workplace transformation is both challenging and exciting. Inventing new ways of approaching existing processes and creating net new business models is powering completely revolutionary industries that will ultimately create a range of as yet undefined career choices. Emerging technologies are creating new industries to provide a growing, evolving portfolio of goods and services. What replaces the iPhone? An AR headset? A brain implant?

Innovative Learning Models Support Career Transformation

Workers will require many new skills to take advantage of the exciting opportunities for twenty-first-century careers. Models for how and where people acquire these skill sets are changing right alongside these morphing business models. In an article in Business Insider, Elon Musk is quoted as saying a college degree isn't required for a job at Tesla. Apple, Google, and Netflix don't require all employees to have four-year degrees either. David Blake, former CEO of Degreed and founder of Future Work Studios, says, "The future doesn't care how you became an expert." All signs point to the need to rethink the learning process, that education is not an event that happened in the past, but rather a life-long journey with lots of different interesting stops along the way.

The global market-driven economy, especially in the US, has a stellar record of supporting innovative companies and entrepreneurs. Investment in research and development over the past century has resulted in inventions that are taken for granted today, such as integrated circuits, personal computers, the Internet and the World Wide Web, mobile phone technology, and GPS to name a few.

This kind of "Innovation Ecosystem" is a critical driver when empowering and supporting workers displaced by technological change. Just as many of today's jobs did not exist a century ago, the careers of the next hundred years are still gestating in the career nebula—they must be nurtured and defined. This new ecosystem will enable workers to acquire the skills needed to move into new roles in entirely new industries.

According to the US Bureau of Labor Statistics, today's college graduates will have eight to ten jobs by the time they are thirty-eight years old. Research indicates that 85 percent of the jobs that today's learners will be doing in the next decade have not been invented yet. They will be using technology that does not exist today to solve problems we don't yet know are problems.

Both a new set of skills and a radically different approach are required. *Improvising Careers* will help you decipher these new models and apply your own unique talents and experiences to be successful in your next job…and the ones after that!

In addition to my "Future Career Toolkit," I also share lessons learned my own nonlinear multimodal path based on eight different and extremely diverse, successful careers spanning over fifty years.

DEVELOPING TWENTY-FIRST CENTURY SKILLS

The rate and pace at which business and global economies are morphing and being disrupted will require that workers have expertise in what some are calling, "twenty-first-century skills."

The worker of the future will need to be:
- A creative problem solver
- Comfortable with ambiguity
- Resourceful and resilient
- Able to work across disciplines
- Aware of their role as a global citizen.

Because the portfolios of innovative and successful companies need to develop and change so rapidly today, smart ones are looking for workers who can connect unlikely dots to help them create products and services that address new and emerging market opportunities. A great interview by *New York Times* writer Thomas Friedman, with the former Google Chief People Officer Laszlo Bock, in 2014 calls out what it takes to be a "Googler"—and it aligns with my perspective.

Rather than acquire a single niche kind of expertise, learners will need to be able to figure out what they need to learn, learn it, apply it, and then do it all again to compete successfully in the new workplace paradigm. These skills and this kind of awareness are table stakes—regardless of age, geographic location, or level of technological prowess. These qualities are increasingly required of workers looking to successfully navigate the new workplace paradigm.

Many universities, including prestigious schools like Harvard and MIT, and smaller academic institutions, are modifying curricula to reflect this rapidly changing workplace. Terrific, skills-specific courseware is now available online from universities and large private sector tech companies like IBM and Amazon, all designed to meet the needs of the rapidly evolving workplace, covering topics ranging from quantum algorithm design to network maintenance.

Improvising Careers is aimed at learners of any age who are contemplating how to facilitate their next career move. The "Future Career Toolkit" is discipline and vertical agnostic; people with a wide range of skills can benefit by applying it. It is worth mentioning that roles ranging from communication to marketing to business development to investment strategy development and more will all be in demand in these new careers, regardless of what business (i.e., vertical or industry) a person is in.

I am excited to provide actionable guidance for those of you who are interested in making a shift—regardless of your age, role or physical location, whether you want to find a way to change direction, or embark on a career that is more fulfilling, more comfortable, more impactful, or more soul-satisfying—whatever your motivating criteria may be.

A land of exciting career opportunities awaits!

– CHAPTER 2 –

Rethinking Work in Modern Times

> "The commute from your bedroom is here to stay."
> —Ladders, Inc. CEO Marc Cenedella[2]

"Civilization both in the East and the West was visited by a destructive plague which devastated nations and caused populations to vanish," historian Ibn Khaldun once said. "It swallowed up many of the good things of civilization and wiped them out."[3]

Sound familiar? No, believe it or not, he's not referencing COVID-19. Khaldun was actually talking about another deadly health crisis in recorded history. Today, we know it as The Black Death.

The Black Death was a bubonic plague that devastated the population of Europe and Asia from 1347 to 1351. Millions of people died, and many more had their lives completely disrupted. Because survivors were exhausted, feeling unfulfilled, and without clear opportunities for advancement in their work, they refused to return to their old jobs. After such a bleak and terrifying ordeal, workers suddenly wanted to focus on creating a better life.

As a result of the life-or-death reality they faced every day, everyone was suddenly forced to pause and rethink their work roles: farm laborers in rural settings, artisans, craftsmen, merchants in urban environments, even the clergy. History indicates that all of them took stock of their lives after a global pandemic had passed, reassessed what they were doing for a living, and asked what it was all worth.

The people who survived The Black Death realized they were part of a system that had limited their ability to succeed; suddenly, the world was opening up with possibilities for *new* kinds of work. People demanded to be paid a living wage and opportunities for successful working roles. The years after The Black Death were recorded as being tumultuous times indeed, but a complete transformation of the workforce occurred as a result.

What Did the Great Resignation Really Represent?

During and towards the end of the pandemic (2020–2022), pundits described a similar trend with many different names: "The Great Resignation" has been a popular name for it. I've also heard "The Big Quit" or "The Great Reshuffle." Whatever you want to call it, people worldwide have been leaving their jobs in historically unprecedented numbers over the past few years.

An article in the Harvard Business Review said that four million Americans quit their jobs in July 2021 alone.[4] Another 2021 article in *The New York Times* stated that "workers are quitting at record rates, indicating that they feel confident about finding new jobs. Wages are growing at rates normally associated with the peak of a boom."[5]

Additionally, a recent survey by Indeed asked employees working remotely full-time how many would quit if their employer required them to return to the office full-time. Thirty-seven percent of remote workers would quit over a Return To Office (RTO) policy![6]

Maybe a Great Rethinking?

And workers were not just quitting because of COVID-19; it seems they were completely reimagining what they wanted out of work and shifting their expectations about professional life. Just as they did in 1351. It seems that many individuals reassessed and decided they wanted a chance to pursue a different career path with different parameters.

Some people realized that they really disliked their jobs. Some realized that their manager was, in fact, a jerk. That there was not enough opportunity for career advancement. That the daily commute was sucking three and four hours a day away from family or personal time. That their employer was not providing clear guidance on training and reskilling. Some were apprehensive about the company's policies to keep them safe during the pandemic.

Hiring recruiters report that 'more work flexibility' has quickly shifted from a perk to an expectation. Lucy Lorenzo, founding partner of Ascension Search Partners, estimated 80 percent to 90 percent of candidates are looking for a position that offers some flexibility.[7] During the pandemic, a story on National Public Radio postulated that "many [people] are rethinking what work means to them, how they are valued, and how they spend their time."[8]

Additionally, for the first time in history, more and more of the population can work whenever they want to and from wherever they are. People are comfortable working from home and, believe it or not, productivity has actually increased, not declined. A study conducted by the University of Chicago gathered data from March 2021 on more than thirty thousand workers who earned at least $20,000. They found that nearly 60 percent reported being more productive working from home than they expected to be, compared with 14 percent who said they got less done.[9]

This is all in sharp contrast to the more traditional workplace climate. Since the 1960s, too many companies have taken a transactional approach to labor, hiring and firing at will to match business needs. There are certainly large, ongoing internal job economies at many major companies (I experienced this up close during my decade and a half working in various roles at IBM, but more on that later). It's just that we, as a society, are starting to see that this model is only a viable and cost-effective option if you have many workers available who can be educated easily using internal resources. And, boy, the times they are a'changin.'

New Ways to Learn and Work

I remember a conversation at an HR event a couple of years ago with a young CEO leading a German omnichannel start-up in Berlin. His concept of providing training was to give each new employee the equivalent of $5,000 and then task them with figuring out how to spend it.

"Take a few classes," he'd tell them. "Attend a conference. Go to a yoga retreat. Learn how to make sushi. Whatever you think will help you advance in the company. You must make those decisions. I won't presume to make them for you!"

This is a terrific model for enabling employee learning and advancement in today's new, emerging workplace.

Today's global market-driven economy requires new processes for acquiring credentials more efficiently. New training models are emerging—not just in brick-and-mortar college classrooms—but also in evolving virtual worlds exploiting the immersive power of technologies like AR and VR; these will be the domains that prepare the next set of workers more quickly and effectively than ever before.

The next generation of the workforce will be more agile regarding skills acquisition. Training will become more self-directed. In fact, I predict that workers will be encouraged to be autodidacts, tasked with figuring out what skills they need and where they can learn them, and then recreating the whole process again for their next career for their entire work life.

Working for "The Man"

Employers must also adopt an innovative approach to the employer/employee relationship. That means focusing more on worker interaction as a relationship, not simply a transactional situation driven by market factors. Today's workers are tired of feeling disposable and want to have a clear sense that the people in charge of their workplace have a vested interest in helping them succeed.

Workers, whether employees or contractors, are now entering new jobs expecting a deserved level of respect. People will not continue in a sucky job they hate; instead, they will look for something more fulfilling. The importance of work-life integration has been brought into clear focus.

More Control, More Flexibility

We've seen many changes in how money is earned through the rise of the gig economy, the increasing number of contingent worker scenarios, and the rapid changes in business opportunities both online and offline. Suddenly, all the lines have blurred. Are we working from home or sleeping in the office? Who knows anymore.

The transitional workforce model being transformed in recent years has been fueled by people discovering that they really liked having the ability to manage and control their own time. And that now they can! It has become an increasingly crucial factor for many workers to determine how they work and how they live their lives more broadly.

The Next Generation

The next generation entering the workforce already has a very different take on what it even means to work. They've grown up using technology in the palm of their hand to connect to information and people around the globe 24/7. Most recently, many were forced to use a virtual world as the only way to attend class, connect with their friends, and even graduate from high school and college as the pandemic raged on in the real world. The "Great Pivot" to a world solely online impacted their formative years in ways we cannot even begin to imagine. So, of course, their view of the workplace and a global society has forever been changed!

Quiet Quitting

I heard a lot of chatter from workforce pundits and armchair economists during and after the pandemic describing a process they say is taking place among younger workers. They are calling it "quiet quitting" which implies that millennial and Gen Z workers are not particularly engaged and are scaling back the amount of time they spend on working hours. Typical reasons offered by their supervisors include "lack of engagement." Others speculate that there's a generation in the workplace that is burned out and recovering from the effects of the pandemic, fighting an apathy fueled by murky paths for advancement, underwhelming training, and unclear career guidance from company leadership.

Personally, I believe many of these are just manufactured knee-jerk explanations for a broader trend. The real reason workers of all ages are dialing back their efforts is much more a reflection of the times. Again, workers want more work-life integration and are much more comfortable effectively juggling multiple gigs than previous generations of workers have been.

I had a conversation not long ago with a young woman working at IBM Corporate Headquarters regarding how she integrated work and life. She said, "Well, I work in a social media role at a Global 100 tech firm during the day, and I design and make clothing at night. Oh, and on the weekends, I am a DJ."

Wow! She's certainly not "quiet quitting." She's setting boundaries and using her range of talents to explore multiple roles that interest her!

This is the reality behind the whole quiet quitting conversation. HR managers and clueless senior executives need to understand that this current shift in attitude cannot simply be explained with, "Kids today (sigh) . . . they are just not interested in work!" The world has evolved, and we've moved into a new era—where what it means to work is very different from what it meant even two or three years ago.

What Do I Think? Well, I'm Glad You Asked . . .

I am reminded of a tale I heard recently where a boomer "busted" a millennial for leaving the office at five p.m. one day.

The boomer sees the millennial packing up her computer and putting on her coat and suddenly gets annoyed.

"Hey, 'New Hire,'" he smirks. "Where do you think you are going, leaving the office at five p.m.? Working a half day today?"

The millennial replies without missing a beat: "Hey, I'm sorry that it takes you forty hours a week to do something I can accomplish in twenty. You should beef up your collaboration skills and use more current technology. See ya!"

Okay, boomer.

Boom.

Mic drop.

And every other thing kids these days are saying . . .

You get the point.

My take on what's going on behind the scenes is that it's really tied to three factors:

1. Younger workers are born with an iPad or iPhone in their hands, so they explore, embrace, and leverage emerging technologies to a much greater degree than boomers and Gen X ever have.
2. Younger workers have grown up with social media and, as a result, are more efficient, more productive, and more collaborative.
3. Younger workers are more focused on work/life integration, rather than being content to just grind it out for thirty years in some mundane job before retiring to *finally have a life.*

What's New Is Old

"Quiet quitting was just a generational twist on an old problem," says Ira Wolfe, workforce thought leader and president at Poised for the Future Co. "Social media took it from HR and business journals to every person's screens."[10]

So then, at a meta-level, this "quiet quitting" approach was an evolving representation of the new models for how people want to work. It's just that simple.

People can get the work done in less time than it took their managers to do it, so they'll do other things with their time. They won't be worker drones feeding the furnace of corporate dictates. They refuse to embrace workforce models put in place years ago when the way businesses operated was completely different.

This workforce transformation is going to continue in the years ahead as the next wave of baby boomers retires and emerging technologies create new opportunities. millennials, followed by Gen Z and then Gen Alpha, will become the dominant workforce demographic and workplace models will inevitably morph.

The Transformation Has Already Begun...

Smart companies are already rethinking how they identify and recruit new workers with skillsets they need. Flexible working schedules make it easier for companies to engage with freelancers and gig workers faster and give them the ability to source talent from all over the globe.

Another trend worth noting is that many traditional organizations are already carving off parts of their businesses to compete with younger, nimbler, tech-driven companies nipping at their heels and stealing market share. They are restructuring into faster, more focused companies in order to keep up with the rapid evolution of the twenty-first century's global market-driven economy.

The implications of this dissolution and reorganizational trend for the evolving workforce are huge and represent tremendous new career opportunities. Take General Electric, for example. A storied company that makes everything from lightbulbs to locomotive engines, GE was the last original member of the Dow Jones Industrial Average to be dropped from the blue-chip index in 2018. Three years later, the company announced that it would split into three different companies focused on healthcare, aviation, and energy. After being a successful, highly regarded global leader for over a century, GE finally determined that splitting up was in the best strategic interests of the business.

Another century-old company made a similar move in October 2021. IBM announced it was carving off its global infrastructure business and renaming it Kyndryl.

These companies are not alone. Others following this dissolution and reorganization model include Toshiba, Johnson & Johnson, Siemens, DowDuPont, and United Technologies. They have all radically modified strategies and go-to-market approaches because of the rapidly changing global business climate.

But just as these highly regarded titans of traditional industry are being sliced and diced, a whole new generation of business giants (read: potential employers) has evolved into what some call "neo-conglomerates." Many have created market caps larger than any company in history; others have diversified their businesses through acquisitions and funded "moonshots" and "skunkworks," just as the historical conglomerates who are now coming unraveled. These include companies like Amazon, Tesla, and Alphabet (Google).

Social media giant Facebook changed its corporate moniker to Meta to rebrand and shift focus from their "cash cow" core business (selling social media advertising) to creating digital, immersive social and business environments.

Once again, the implications for today's workforce are huge. There will be opportunities at the neo-conglomerates and at the broken-off pieces of the older businesses. To be successful, these companies will be required to adopt and exploit new technologies that will create new jobs to address new market demands, while also addressing the need for flexibility in global business models.

Why This Matters Now

Finally, talented people are being given many more options regarding how and where they make a living. You, dear reader, are uniquely positioned to take advantage of this new paradigm. We are in the beginning stages of a once-in-a-generation opportunity for people to reflect and change direction in their lives and careers.

Today, people want to do a job they like—not just something to earn a paycheck. Some want to start their own businesses. Others want to totally shift gears and go from a corporate setting to a nonprofit. Or move to a role that has a broader socio-cultural impact, like working for a firm focused on addressing climate change or food insecurity. Or engage a passion for addressing healthcare challenges on a global scale. Or step up and learn a totally unexpected set of skills and move to a completely new and unlikely role.

One objective in authoring this book is to help people, regardless of age, better understand how companies will interact with the workforce in this new era and what it means to work. By exploring how business models are evolving and by providing a set of Future Career tools, this book can enable you to succeed in the new workplace paradigm. (Details in Chapters 9–11.)

It All Comes Down to This...

The bottom line for today's workers is that there is lots of interesting work and many interesting problems to solve. The tables have turned, and employees, contractors, and gig workers are in the driver's seat. I anticipate that everything I've mentioned in this chapter will create workplace settings that will provide you with new and exciting careers in the years to come.

People of all ages who understand this emerging transformation of the worker/company relationship will succeed in the emerging workplace models. This book can help you find the job/career that really makes you feel fulfilled today, and enable you to track down your next one after that.

Overall, the strategies I'm about to share can help you succeed in moving from a job you do for a living to a sequence of careers that excite and enrich you.

– CHAPTER 3 –

Carving Spears to Writing Algorithms

> "I refuse to issue a patent on a mechanized knitting machine for fear it will put my poor subjects out of work."
> —Queen Elizabeth I, 1589

HOW WORK HAS EVOLVED OVER THE CENTURIES

One of my favorite quotes about the evolution of work comes from Queen Elizabeth I and is cited in Steven Rattner's *The New York Times* article "Fear Not the Coming of The Robots."[11] The article and the quote provide a historical perspective to help us think about the current transformation of the job economy and the modern workplace.

Even way back in the first Queen Elizabeth's day, some 430 years ago, people were nervous about new trends taking jobs away from workers and technology transforming how people earned a living. As time marched on, a group calling themselves "The Luddites"[12] reacted to those concerns by forming an organization that destroyed knitting machinery as a form of protest. In the Luddites' world, the work people in that era had been doing at home—spinning, cleaning, dying the wool—was suddenly being moved into factories to be done by machines. They believed that the machines were a fraudulent way to get around the labor practices of the day. Some would say it all worked out in the end: the companies that created the mills hired townspeople to run the machines, "lifting all proverbial boats" from an economic perspective.

However, people today have similar fears about the impact of technologies like robots and automation on the current workplace. I recently heard a relevant anecdote about DHL, the global package delivery company. A woman there described people who formerly were monitoring packages gliding along on conveyor belts as now performing the job of "robot wranglers"—setting up protocols and processes to enable robots to do the work that humans used to do as efficiently and productively as possible.

This is just one example of a workplace process that has been reinvented and reimagined to adopt the current technology options. It joins a long list of transitional moments that have occurred for centuries . . . if not longer.

The Ice Age Workforce

The concept of work has been evolving right along with human evolution for literally thousands of years. At some point a long time ago, our ancestors' main job every day was to exit the cave, stalk the largest animal they could find, kill it, and then drag it back to where the rest of the crew was huddled. This was, as they say, "all in a day's work."

In fact, the range of skills needed for a successful team in the workforce of 100,000 B.C.E. might have included:

- **"Spear Designer and Craftsman"** makes lightweight but sturdy spears with sharp ends capable of piercing an animal hide.
- **"Hunt Javelinist"** throws the spear; must have a strong arm and good distance vision.
- **"Hunt Coordinator"** possesses solid knowledge of local terrain to figure out where the wild beasts are roaming.
- **"Hunt Transportation Team"** drags or carries the hunt's outcome back to the family/clan; must have strength skills enough to haul heavy freight long distances.
- **"Field Dresser/Butcher"** skins and dresses the game for consumption.
- **"Fashion Designer"** makes comfortable and functional clothing from the animal hide.
- **"Combustion Supervisor"** builds and maintains a fire for cooking, a plus if the subject is sufficient in overall cave heating and cooling skills.
- **"Hunt Residual Manager and Merchandising Specialist"** maps out how to use the rest of the animal for bedding, footwear, artwork, and other applications.

Obviously, these titles are a bit tongue-in-cheek. But today, we have similar supervisors and specialists managing algorithms and robots who do work that used to take hours of back-breaking labor or migraine-inducing statistical analysis. Machines help us accomplish tasks at a level and pace unimaginable just a few years ago. But this is just part of a pattern that has been transforming work for a long time throughout history.

Let's back up for a minute. What does it even mean to work? There are many theories out there from social scientists to economists to academics to ethnographers to corporate business leaders.

According to the Online Etymology Dictionary, the word "work" is derived from the Old English "weorc or worc," meaning an act performed by someone; or labor performed in some useful or profitable way. In ancient Norse, it was "verk," and Old High German speakers called it "werah."[13] Whatever the language, people have been doing jobs for centuries in one way or another.

The Emergence of the Marketplace

In his book *Team Human,* Douglas Rushkoff describes an important turning point in the concept of work that foreshadows our current situation.[14] He believes today's work world resulted from the idea of the marketplace (or "the bazaar") brought back from the Middle East and introduced to Medieval Europe by the Crusaders.

European Crusaders witnessed firsthand how Middle Eastern farmers grew crops that they would then bring to sell at a central location near an urban population center. Local craftsmen and artisans soon did the same. As a result, the bazaar was a rich marketplace for trading goods and skills. At the time, this was a totally alien concept in a European society where peasants worked for nobles and had few ways to generate income other than serving at the will of the lords and ladies.

On the other hand, the marketplace bazaar presented a way to level the playing field and give people the ability to monetize their skills and get compensated for what they knew how to do. The way we use this model has been evolving for hundreds of years, but at the end of the day, people and organizations still make stuff to sell—both goods *and* services. In fact, this marketplace work model has been recreated in the digital world in the early twenty-first century. Think of digital marketplaces for services like UpWork and Fiverr or ones for selling products like Etsy or Weebly.

Work, Work, Work

Long after the days of the Middle Eastern bazaar and the European marketplaces, the twentieth-century transition from a farming culture to a more industrialized one took place over the course of about one hundred years. The chief organizational breakthrough of the Industrial Revolution in the United States was the development of the "factory system," where work was performed on a large scale in a single centralized location.[15]

The types of jobs people did for money changed because of technical innovation at the time. For example, many turn-of-the-century farriers and blacksmiths eventually learned to become auto mechanics after Henry Ford started cranking out Model Ts from his factories in Detroit in 1908. In 1790, farmers made up 90 percent of the US population. By 1920, that number had dropped to 30 percent. The Industrial Revolution, of course, was a catalyst for this transition.[16]

Technological innovations have also upended what were once considered standard practices, and, for the most part, we're thankful for them. Take innovations in health care or transportation, for example. Would you want to go back to biting a bullet as they sawed off your leg after being on the wrong side of a horse and wagon accident? Or would you want to spend six weeks on a wobbly sailing ship to get from New York to London? Or just imagine needing thirty days to have a message created in Boston be delivered in San Francisco!

The Age of Information

Today's solutions, like virtual reality-assisted surgery, intercontinental jet travel, and instant messaging, would all seem like science fiction to a visitor from the 18th century. We now find ourselves in what anthropologists call the "The Age of Information," or "The Fourth Industrial Revolution." Changes have been driven by business needs as well as cultural shifts, and the changes have been led by inventive, non-traditional thinkers and creators—much like you, dear reader.

As we sit here in the early decades of the twenty-first century, the world is changing dramatically regarding what it *even means to work.* Emerging trends represented by the "gig economy" are upending the traditional ways that employers and employees historically interacted. In turn, this has changed the way value is created and distributed. Many of us work in the "knowledge economy" every day, sitting at our computers or thumb-typing into our smartphones. It's rapidly becoming the standard model for much of the global workforce. Inevitably, this will also dictate the skills you need to get paid for your talent and experience.

Automation and Value Creation

In 2013, two Oxford professors estimated that 47 percent of US jobs are at "risk" of automation. On the other hand, researchers at the University of Mannheim suggest that only 9 percent of jobs have the potential to be eliminated by machines. Another study by the Organization for Economic Co-Operation and Development suggests that number might actually be around 14 percent, but at the same time, states an additional "32 percent of jobs have a risk of between 50 percent and 70 percent, pointing to the possibility of significant change in the way these jobs are carried out as a result of automation."[17]

So, expert opinion on this topic tends to vary.

But we do know for certain that things are being automated more and more. So, work is evolving into activities that only humans are good at—things like understanding other people, thinking creatively, dealing with ambiguity, and being resourceful when solving problems. This allows companies to shift the focus of their outcomes from cost reduction and efficiency to the acceleration of value creation.

To accomplish value creation, people need to think about how creativity and imagination are expressed in different contexts. For example, when people say only a certain kind of person is creative, we need to start by widening the definition of just what creativity really is and how it can be applied in various settings. Every business out there—from financial services to scrapbooking—requires a unique kind of creativity and imagination for the person doing it to be successful. Exceptional creative skills will no doubt be increasingly seen as the qualities that set people apart for working in jobs that don't exist yet.

The basic criteria for success in jobs that don't exist yet, though, are even broader. They encompass what Silicon Valley entrepreneur and author John Hagel calls "capabilities" or "being able to do things that will have value in any environment."[18]

These include qualities like curiosity, imagination, creativity, emotional intelligence, and social intelligence—all essential skills for addressing unseen problems and opportunities regardless of the environment.

Frankly, these qualities are tough for machines to deliver.

We also must remember the historical perspective. These changes have been going on for centuries, which is not a bad thing. It just means that people will once again have to learn how to design, develop, enhance, and maintain a new set of marketable skills.

Nowadays, the knowledge economy allows us to work wherever we are and accomplish whatever whenever we need to have it done. And the COVID-19 pandemic reinforced this approach. As I noted earlier, fewer and fewer people are commuting to traditional office settings. More and more people are adopting the model of "if you can get online, you *are* at work" whether in a coffee shop, on a train, in an airport lounge, or in your pajamas sitting on your bed with your laptop. In other words, technology is making geography history.

What's the Big Idea?

Capturing *ideas and concepts* into a digital framework or deliverable is key to what a client is willing to pay for, both today and in the future, because it generates attributable revenue, which keeps consumers and shareholders happy. Some of the output is in the form of physical objects (like smartphones, jetliners, buildings, rockets, Mars helicopters, self-monitoring exoskeletons, or robots). Other work products are more intangible: research findings, insightful blogs, captivating images, and high-quality videos or animation.

What differentiates a product or service in the marketplace is much more intangible. It's the *functionality* the output delivers. In other words, what's the 'real world' use? Delivering this kind of value requires new and evolving skills and is part of an accelerating trend, as you may already know. In short, future workers must be aware of this and embrace it to succeed. (More detail on this in Chapter 5: Getting Down to Busine$$.)

Easy Come, Easy Go

The indisputable fact is jobs come, and jobs go. Career options appear, morph, some disappear, and then others emerge, transformed by technology and culture. The optimistic takeaway from this insight is that there will always be work in one form or another. Media guru and author Tim O'Reilly once declared, "We won't run out of work until we run out of problems."[19]

Enough said.

– CHAPTER 4 –

Brace Yourself for a Future of Solar Sails and Ingestible Robots

IT'S *ALWAYS* ABOUT TECHNOLOGY

One perspective that we always need to keep in mind when discussing the future of work and careers is the impact of technology. We need to think more broadly about what exactly this concept encompasses. As we discussed in the last chapter, technological advancements have driven humankind's transformation and evolution for thousands of years, so it's important to take a step back and remind ourselves of the historical arc of tech development that has brought us to where we are today.

At the risk of being overly simplistic, the pace at which technology transforms skill needs has been accelerating for literally thousands of years. The time between building a fire in your cave and the creation of the Franklin Stove is probably in the range of ten thousand years. The shift from non-AI-supported content creation to the use of ChatGPT took place in about a month. Get ready to embrace an ever-increasing pace of tech emergence and adoption and its career implications.

Early humankind developed tech-driven innovations that enabled them to tame fire, make a wheel, create horseshoes, build durable shelters, create tools made of stone and metal, and design communication solutions using everything from clay tablets to papyrus scrolls. The impact of technology, of course, includes even more complex science-driven solutions throughout history like the printing press, compass, telescope, steam locomotive, and automobile.

Even the concept of paper money, introduced by Kublai Khan, a grandson of the great conqueror Genghis in 1260, can be viewed as a technological example.[20] It is, at its core, an application for storing and distributing value. Of course, today we use Bitcoin, Ethereum, Dogecoin and other cryptoassets to accomplish the same basic objective.

From Abacus to Apple Watch

From the perspective of specific tools designed to perform complex calculations quickly and easily, we have transformed and evolved solutions for thousands of years to address this specific kind of challenge. Consider the abacus, an ancient calculating machine. This simple device consists of beads that move up and down across poles in a frame—often made of wood or metal. It is thought to have originated five thousand years ago in Babylon.[21]

The next historical number-crunching tool came from Charles Babbage, considered by some to be the "father of the computer." In the 1820s, he proposed the idea of the "Difference Engine," a mechanical calculating machine that could add, subtract, multiply, and divide. An early working model was powered by cranking a handle.[22]

Our next stop in the history of calculating machines is the University of Pennsylvania in the 1940s where ENIAC (Electronic Numerical Integrator and Computer) made its debut. The press dubbed it a "Giant Brain," and it took up an entire fifty-by-thirty-foot room. ENIAC was the first large-scale computer to run at electronic speed leveraging vacuum tubes, not "hindered by mechanical parts." Until a 1955 lightning strike, ENIAC is believed to have run more calculations than all of humanity had done up to that point in time. It could calculate a ballistic trajectory in thirty seconds that would have taken a human twenty hours to complete.[23]

Quantum Leap

Fast-forward to September 2019. Google's Sycamore 54 qubit quantum computer performed a calculation in two hundred seconds that would have required a classical computer ten thousand years to complete. The machine had achieved what has been called "quantum supremacy": the ability of a quantum-mechanics-based machine to perform a calculation that would basically be impossible for a traditional classical computer to execute.[24]

Recently, Chinese researchers claimed to have built a 56-qubit machine that can perform operations that are orders of magnitude faster than Google's quantum computer, its closest competitor. The Chinese quantum computer completed a complex calculation in a little over an hour, a task that would take a classical supercomputer like IBM's Summit *eight years* to perform.[25]

Work and Tech

Obviously, technology is continuing to drive breathtaking upheavals in every aspect of civilization and society. Innovations like virtual reality, suborbital vehicles, implanted sensors, and AI-enabled robots are completely disrupting education, communication, health care, and travel. To paraphrase author Thomas Friedman, we are experiencing the "ongoing flattening of the planet," soon to be followed by the solar system and then the entire universe.[26]

We could see humans on Mars within a decade, find new sources of renewable energy, witness the eradication of cancer, explore tourism on the Moon, develop 3D-printed prosthetics and body parts controlled by brainwaves, and make autonomous drone vehicles commonplace. Your neighbor could be a genetically engineered human! There are technologies and innovative solutions coming soon that we can barely imagine now.

Think of recent companies that have upended historical business models by leveraging technology. In 2020, Uber was the largest taxi and limousine company globally, but it doesn't own any cars.[27] As of November 2021, Airbnb was worth more than Marriott, Hilton, and Hyatt combined (according to the website Seeking Alpha). Yet they don't own any real estate.[28] This has broad implications for skills, jobs, and careers.

What This Means for You

The exciting news is that this is the proverbial 'perfect storm' connecting new business models with innovative technologies, the likes of which we have never seen before. And these will inevitably drive new and unimagined career opportunities.

The evaluation and analysis of the *skills marketplace* is laying the groundwork for this tremendously powerful new ability to connect business drivers with skill needs. Combine this with the almost unlimited access to all kinds of learning assets available to the general public, and the result is an evolving ecosystem that will transform how we live and work.

Work's Future

This transformation of the workplace specifically is only going to continue to accelerate. MIT Professor and author Thomas Malone predicts that over the course of the next decade, corporations will devolve into a small set of resources with discipline-specific skills: marketing, strategy, operations, legal etc.[29] Their role will be organizing and oversight. Every other business process will be managed using networks, much the way movies are made.

Let me explain what I mean. I was recently an extra on the set of a Netflix film called, *The Noel Diary*. (Yes, I am a member of the Screen Actors Guild—I did a TV movie with Peter O'Toole and several episodes of the soap opera All My Children back in the day!) It was incredible and very eye-opening to see the movie-making process up close! The different skill sets involved all worked together in a seamless dance to achieve a singular objective. It was just amazing: from the director to the crew putting up reflective panels, to the swarms of wardrobe personnel, to artists roaming among us between takes to tweak our make-up to the actors reciting their lines. The range of energy and focus and talent was remarkable.

Could modern corporations move as efficiently and creatively as that? The world would certainly be a better place! In the future, I believe this same approach will apply to everything, from building a submarine to designing a smartphone app. There will be groups—subsets of the network—with specific skills, each of whom will work with other groups using their own set of specific skills to create a final deliverable or product. Discipline-specific teams will form and disband depending on any specific work situation's needs.

In this new workplace model, people will have much more flexibility when it comes to taking a job or engaging in a project to make sure it aligns with their values and worldview. In today's corporate setting, you sometimes have to just suck it up and do what you're told without any input. In the new model, however, workers will have the freedom to decline a job that requires them to support a company that is negatively impacting the environment or exploiting underpaid workers in emerging markets or does not have a robust focus on diversity and inclusion and gender parity.

Of course, this new marketplace will require workers to be hyper-connected and constantly monitor what skills are in demand. Workers will need to be vigilant about what gaps may exist in their own skill sets that they must address in order to stay viable (read: get paid).

But the good news is that people of all ages who are willing to learn, adapt, and acquire new skills can get paid. This future workplace will offer opportunities that are not specific to one's level of education, geographical location, gender, or age.

Talkin' 'Bout Communication

We now have the tools such as chat, text, email, video, laptops, smartphones, which enable us to communicate and work instantaneously. People anywhere on the planet can interact with each other in real time. Virtual reality is in the process of transforming our options for interaction even more dramatically, enabling digital immersive experiences that will make Zoom calls feel like a throwback to another era. Facebook is even concentrating on Metaverse environments where we can all interact, work, and play via *disembodied avatars.*

At no time since humans began tramping around the surface of Terra Firma and wandering through the Pleistocene wilderness have we seen a transformation of such magnitude. Technology is now enabling the accelerated creation of value, the sharing of unconnected ideas, and the evolution of social and business concepts on a global scale. We are entering the Age of Enlightenment 2.0.

The net takeaway is that technology drives human progress and, by association, business models, skills-in-demand, and careers that happen as a result. Every company today is a technology company, whether they like it or not. Let's face it: any other approach these days is practically a "going out of business" strategy. Think about what happened to companies like Eastman Kodak, Blockbuster, Tower Records, and Borders Books Stores. (Many of you may even be asking, "Eastman Who?"). These companies and business models missed the signals that times and technology were changing. The tech changed, but they didn't. Oops!

So, it's important to embrace the tech you have access to today while keeping in mind that it will change, morph, and evolve. It's essential for you to be prepared to embrace the next set of mind-blowing advances. And the one(s) after that, and the one(s) after that and . . . well, you get the idea.

– CHAPTER 5 –

Getting Down to Busine$$

As we discovered in the last chapter, new technologies drive innovative business models, which have consistently improved people's overall lives for centuries. The evolution of jobs coming and going is driven by the basic premise that we live in a world of market-driven global economics.

A great resource on this topic is a book called *Technological Revolutions and Financial Capital* by Carlota Perez, a Venezuelan economist and professor at the London School of Economics. Perez describes a series of five transitions that have happened over the past 450 years, all driven by technological innovations. She also explores how, ultimately, money, and by implication, jobs and careers—have been connected to all of them. She describes the process as basically a "structurally engineered system of collapse and reward." [30]

The cycles she describes include:
- The Industrial Revolution.
- The Age of Steam and Railways.
- The Age of Steel, Electricity, and Heavy Engineering.

- The Age of Oil, Automobiles, and Mass Production.
- The Age of Information.

But how does all this historical context connect to being successful at jobs that don't exist yet?

Well, innovative companies are driven by the constant changes taking place across the global marketplace. Today, successful companies constantly evolve their portfolios of products and services much faster than they used to over the past 150 years. Organizations create, update, and revise their offerings at a rapidly increasing pace. Let's face it: the market *and consumers* demand more and more stuff faster and faster.

Consumers want the latest social media app, the 'smartest' smartphone, the best drone, and the fastest streaming service, and they want it all yesterday. Increasing market pressure requires companies to evolve quickly to stay viable and profitable, attract talent, and keep Wall Street appeased.

Because of this, employees, gig workers, and freelancers alike will need the ability to pivot and adjust to create, sell, market, and support. Workers will be required to learn, unlearn, and relearn all kinds of skills, some of which are obvious and others we can't even imagine. A company's "workforce" must be adaptive, flexible, resilient, and self-directed to stay competitive and gainfully employed. There will, of course, be varying degrees of transferable skills, but there will also always be a need to learn net new ones as well.

Why Do Jobs Change?
Let's go back to an example we touched on in the previous chapter: the adoption of automobiles and the

manufacturing assembly line in the 1900s. When Henry Ford's Model Ts started rolling out of his factory in Detroit in 1908, many in the horse-and-carriage business were understandably in a panic.[31] Those once valued and well-paying skills were suddenly obsolete.

Yet I have no doubt that smart workers leveraged their understanding of horse-drawn wagon construction, identified the skills gaps, and then acquired the needed skills to make the leap to a whole new career. For example, carriage makers with experience building vehicles pulled by horses learned how to incorporate a new propulsion system, the internal combustion engine. By transferring existing skills and acquiring new ones, they could continue to be gainfully employed in the new workplace model.

Similar transformative processes have happened since then and continue to disrupt work models. But they always represent new career opportunities.

The personal computer or laptop has replaced the typewriter. Wall Street traders are being replaced by algorithms. Live musicians are being supplanted by digital samples and loops. Libraries piled high from floor to ceiling with books have been replaced by Wikipedia and Google searches. Artificial Intelligence is now creating paintings and replacing workers in a variety of fields, from radiology to accounting.

It Takes a Village: Adjacent Industries and the Supply Chain

While breakthrough technologies and innovations drive job creation directly, you must always remember, dear reader, that job and career opportunities always emerge as an added benefit from these changes. Take, for example, the invention and subsequent adoption of the railroad, something we probably don't think about much today. I, for example, can jump on any number of Metro-North trains and be in New York City in less than an hour. Or I can book an Amtrak seat and arrive at MIT in Cambridge after only a few hours' ride along the Eastern seaboard shoreline. Or I can get to Washington, DC or Chicago or even San Francisco by driving down to JFK or La Guardia and jumping on a plane

But in the mid-1830s, a new technology, the *steam locomotive,* had just arrived on the scene and was poised to disrupt how people and goods moved from one location to another.[32] Folks in the transportation business who used to make money moving goods around with horse-drawn wagons started to realize that the age of "The Iron Horse" had arrived. Simply put, the railroad held the potential to have a transformational effect on business, society, and culture. Soon, discussions took place around a variety of connected topics such as:

- How long should the railroad cars be?
- What spacing between the rails is best?
- Does it make sense to move just products, or will people want to travel on this new-fangled contraption, too?
- Who will provide support services like storing and loading coal and water into the engines?

- What new skills will be needed for locomotive engineers, conductors, mechanics, construction crews, architects, and cleaning crews?

Driven by economic factors, shipping freight was the initial focus of the new locomotive industry, but eventually, people wanted to use this new mode of transportation to just go for a joy ride, travel to a vacation destination, maybe visit friends and family, or explore the world. So then comfortable passenger accommodations evolved, and eventually, travelers could enjoy the view of the country whizzing past from luxury dining cars or Pullman coaches for sleeping on long trips.

Think of how business changed then: one company might have made the seats and upholstery for the railroad cars. Trains also needed windows, carpeting, rolling kitchens, and dining facilities. Chefs would have to learn new skills, too: no one had ever sliced into a medium-rare Porterhouse going seventy-five miles an hour at night through Indiana before!

Yes, this innovative technology allowed workers to leverage a certain set of transferable skills. But it also required everyone to rethink and reapply their skills in a brand-new *context*. Lighting, heating, cooling, cooking, and cleaning—these were all services needed in this new rolling, non-location-specific mobile environment.

However, these "railroad-specific" challenges and opportunities were just one aspect of the job creation engine driven by the adoption of the steam locomotive. The railroad also drove the development of many very specific adjacent businesses. The development of portable, accurate timepieces is a prime example.

Efficient rail transportation demanded an accurate and consistent time-keeping system. As railroads began to reduce the travel time between cities from days and weeks to mere hours, towns having their own "local" time made for a scheduling nightmare. This led to many changes as regards how humans think of and measure time. One of the first solutions after time zones were adopted in 1883 was the development of what became known as the "railroad" watch.[33]

Created to deliver precision and durability, these timepieces were once important tools used by various professionals. My Great-Uncle Douglas, for example, used to proudly show me his timepiece from when he worked for the New York Central Railroad in the 1930s and 1940s. Eventually, watches became cheap enough to be made available to the general public, but it took many years. It happened much the same way computers went from room-sized machines accessible only to a few at businesses and universities to today's world where we all have the ability *to strap one to our wrist* or carry it in our bag in phone or tablet form.

Back to the railroad example, many other jobs began springing up to support the new business model that was evolving. Redcaps helped passengers haul their luggage on and off the train. Conductors strolled through the cars, taking tickets. Engineers drove the locomotives. Companies provided coal and water for the steam engines.

Today, the model for this kind of evolution has not changed much; only the specific needs are different. Just as locomotives needed water and coal then, quantum computers today need dilution refrigerators and wiring harnesses. By implication, even more new careers are born that are directly connected to both the supplemental and core business.

A recent article in the *Wall Street Journal* makes my point very powerfully.[34] As the adoption of electric vehicles continues to accelerate (pun intended), the automobile industry is undergoing upheaval. Companies in the supply chain that have made various kinds of parts for gas engines are now scrambling to reinvent themselves. And, of course, they are encountering unlikely new competitors from major electronics companies like LG and Panasonic, who make batteries and other parts for plug-in vehicles.

"We don't want to be left making the best buggy whips," said Chris Wallbank, chief executive of P.J. Wallbank Springs, Inc., an auto supplier in Port Huron, Michigan. For forty years, his company made one part: a spring for automatic transmissions that historically was used in roughly 10 million new vehicles every year. But most *electric* vehicles do not have geared transmissions. Mr. Wallbank says he is now looking for candidates interested in a business development role to determine if his company's product can be adapted for electric vehicle use.[35]

Do You Want a Case With That Smartphone?

Take a moment and think about the vast number of adjacent businesses that have sprung up to support the ongoing development of a technology we probably take for granted today: the smartphone. Everyone needs a case and maybe a screen protector. Everyone has to have a cable to charge their device. Most of us then use apps to buy things, do our banking, and keep up with the latest news, sports, and celebrity gossip. Perhaps you even have an external backup battery in case you run out of juice on the beach or on a long trip. The list goes on and on.

There are dozens, if not *hundreds,* of companies fulfilling these needs and making a profit doing so, and these businesses need skilled, talented workers like you to help them grow for whatever new technology is coming next.

Regardless of where it was developed or how it is applied, there will always be adjacent profit opportunities to support existing products as they are developed. Some of these opportunities will be seized by large corporations, and others will be addressed by niche start-ups. But these changes always become a powerful driver of the next set of career opportunities.

The Darwinism of Skills

Companies, both today and in the future, are increasingly looking for people who can demonstrate emergent leadership, as well as create new opportunities for revenue. New business models will continue to emerge in every discipline, whether it is communication, travel and transportation, media and entertainment, healthcare, education, legal services, energy production, and so on. This means you need to be alert, always keeping in mind that, while current models might be successful, things inevitably change.

The basic message here is that the concept of jobs and careers has been in flux since the days of hunting and gathering. And the changes are always driven by advances in technology. All a company has to do to make money is create something the market wants. The challenge is that the changes are happening faster than they ever have in human history.

But this only means that more and more new skills will be in demand. This also means there is a wide range of exciting new career opportunities just ahead for today's learners, and they will be found in jobs that don't exist yet.

– CHAPTER 6 –

Connect the Dots

INVESTIGATING THE INTERSECTION OF UNLIKELY DISCIPLINES

One of the nicest compliments I ever received was from someone at a global consortium of prestigious independent schools. I had given a keynote address at the Texas STEAM Summit in Houston, and the Director of Curriculum at Nord Anglia, a network of private schools, came up to me afterwards.

"I go to many conferences where the speaker says that today's learners will be doing jobs that don't exist today. And then the speaker declares that they have *no idea* what those jobs will be," he told me with a smile. "But you talked about very specific jobs and careers that are emerging that are very tangible. More importantly, you shared a perspective on how kids can really think about what kinds of skills they are going to need to pursue these new careers."

I was flattered. What really had made such an impression on him was that I named half a dozen possible jobs of the future, all based on various indicators that pop up when I'm looking at business trends, investment opportunities, patent filings, tech innovations, and other sources.

To be honest, I do not think any of my strategies are exactly brain surgery. There are many ways to get a sense of what's coming next in the world of work. You can analyze past models for value creation, such as what kinds of products and services companies have been making and selling over the past decades. And you can also look at the ways in which new technologies are creating exciting new opportunities.

Again, careers are typically driven by economic factors, and they have historically evolved at the intersection of the old and the new. Business models appear, morph, and disappear. Successful ideas leverage existing technologies and combine them with emerging approaches or processes. Think again to our earlier discussion about the transition of the horse-and-buggy business to the brand-new automobile, or "horseless carriage." The name virtually says it all.

A Victorian-Era Genius Gave Us Smartphones ... Wait ... What?

James Maxwell is one of my favorite examples of a person who saw two disciplines that hadn't been connected, then researched and defined just exactly how they *were*, in fact, *connected*. Maxwell lived, wrote, and taught in Scotland and England way back in the middle of the nineteenth century. Today, he is primarily known as the scientist who revolutionized not only physics, but to be honest, from our vantage point a century and a half later, how much of how the planet functions.

His groundbreaking paper, "A Dynamical Theory of the Electromagnetic Field," was published in 1865, and it laid the groundwork for rethinking how electricity and magnetism operated together. Even though he lived in a time when people lit their homes with gas lamps, he developed innovative theories for the foundation of the global electrical power grid, digital communications, the Internet, MRIs, GPS, Bluetooth, computers, smartphones, and so on. Basically, his theories underpin the energy and communications infrastructure upon which *the entire world now depends.* (Incidentally, aside from this work, Maxwell *also* investigated the rings of Saturn and helped develop processes for early color photography!)[36] More about how you, dear reader, can explore multiple areas of interest is ahead in Chapter 7: Think Like a Genius.

In the late 1800s, Thomas Edison and his team explored Maxwell's theories, and the result was being able to flip a switch and fill a dark room with light by 1879.[37] Guglielmo Marconi used the same theories in 1901 to transmit radio waves—the lowest form of electromagnetic energy—across the Atlantic Ocean.[38] In more recent times—whether he knew it or not—Steve Jobs stood on Maxwell's shoulders when he created the first iPhone in 2007.[39]

Obviously, James Maxwell's "connecting the dots" approach to innovation has influenced society and culture in profound ways. And, by using these same macro approaches, you, too, will be empowered to transform society, business, and culture in the years ahead.

"Orphans Preferred"—Pony Express Recruitment Poster

Speaking of iPhones, another major communications breakthrough occurred in 1860 when four bankers in St. Louis came up with a brilliant idea to accelerate content being transported across the continent. Back then, it typically took thirty days for a message to get from New York to San Francisco. That seems almost impossible to believe today. These days, we can share a feeling, an image, an insight, or a meme instantaneously with anyone anywhere on the planet, and we measure interaction lag time in milliseconds. But, back in the 1800s, high-speed communication was measured in months.

So, the St. Louis bankers came up with an idea to hire a bunch of young horsemen to ride as fast as they could through the often-dangerous Western territories carrying letters and other packages. If you can believe it, their recruiting poster actually said, *"Orphans Preferred."* The bankers set up way stations where the riders could swap horses every ten miles or so, and they called their communications network "The Pony Express."

Hundreds of young men jumped at the opportunity, and the Pony Express grew quickly. This innovative solution had combined humans, horses, and way stations in a previously unconnected manner to accelerate message delivery across the country. In fact, the Pony Express had a profound impact on commerce as well as communication. It shortened the cycle time for getting contracts executed, real estate deals completed, and payments delivered. Person A in NYC could suddenly share family news, love letters, or money with Person B in San Francisco in only ten days! The pace was unimaginable at the time.

Lightning in a Bottle

However, their business model was soon threatened by new technological breakthroughs. First came the "Victorian Internet"—otherwise known as the telegraph—developed in the 1830s and 1840s by Samuel Morse and other inventors.[40] By 1861, there were telegraph lines stretching from the East to the West coast of the US. This fact alone suddenly allowed almost instantaneous communication between the two sides of the country.

At first, the St. Louis bankers behind The Pony Express thought they could compete with the telegraph because they delivered *physical* content, like contracts, money, stock certificates, small durable goods, etc. After all, the telegraph—since there were no printers at the time—could only transmit information that someone sent at one end of the line for another person to write down at the other end. Then, the completion of the first transcontinental railroad a few years later made quick cross-country transportation of people and goods possible for the first time. Now, people had the means to physically move objects quickly and securely from one side of the country to the other.

This combination of technologies delivered innovative alternatives that addressed a market need. But it also resulted in catastrophe for older, specialized solutions: Bye, Bye,

Pony Express. The company stopped service just two days after Western Union completed its telegraph lines across the continent in 1861. In short, the Pony Express had a market monopoly for nineteen months, and then they were gone.[41]

Ride, Baby, Ride

A similar transformation occurred in the transportation business early in the twentieth century. As we discussed earlier, horseless carriages were all the rage. Soon, innovations such as the electric starter had improved gas engines, and large batteries were tough to come by for early electric vehicles. Gasoline engines eventually won out, in part because of Henry Ford's assembly-line innovations.

Henry Ford took the basic paradigm of a vehicle that had historically used horses to move people and goods and replaced the animal with an internal combustion engine (combining old and new technology to create a new one!) His first automobile used *bicycle tires* because they could give a smoother, more comfortable ride than the wooden wheels that were typically used on horse-drawn vehicles. Ford used a time-tested and culturally accepted transportation model as his starting point and then transformed it. And, because of that, he was able to basically reinvent the way humans and their stuff moved across the surface of the planet.[42]

This also provides a great example of how careers were disrupted by new innovations. When cars started rolling off the assembly line, people with a certain range of skills (carriage makers, blacksmiths, street sweepers cleaning up horse droppings, stable boys, harness makers…and on and on) suddenly had to improvise. The smart ones took the skills that were *transferable,* figured out what new skills they needed and then made a new path. They connected the dots to new opportunities.

As I mentioned before, carriage makers, for example, knew how to make carriages. But with that demand suddenly gone, maybe they learned how to repair internal combustion engines to stay employable. Maybe some opened gas stations. Blacksmiths could maybe open auto repair shops.

In short, this is the model you must keep in mind, dear reader, as you navigate your multiple careers: use the skills you have, figure out what skill you need to learn to roll with changing technology, find out where you can learn it, and then learn it. And then do this over and over again throughout your career(s).

Let's Gaze into the Crystal Ball...

An emerging discipline called *nanopharmacy* is a good example of how modern technologies and existing ones will meld in the near future. In 2016, three chemists won the Nobel Prize for developing a set of machines that can operate at the nanoscale (10-9, for all you math geeks out there).[43] Nanoscale technology itself is a rapidly growing field that has the potential to impact many different business models. But combine that with the increasing ability to create and refine *pharmacology* at the molecular and even atomic level and you have a whole new set of career options!

A recent example is called *neural dust,* a piece of gear the size of a grain of rice that can be implanted in a patient. This incredible technology can not only monitor various physiological functions, but also stimulate tissue using safe, low-power ultrasound.[44]

These two disciplines are poised to merge in new and exciting ways! Companies are already developing a variety of nanomachines. Students are learning mechanical engineering skills at the nanoscale. Numerous chemists, drug makers, and pharmacologists are working on innovations at the nanoscale level, too. In fact, by creating very specific medicines using tools like CRISPR DNA-editing technology and 3D printing, we will soon be able to deliver drugs to very targeted and specific locations in the human body—directly to a wound or tumor for example. The implications are mind-blowing![45]

I, Robot

As robots and algorithms become more embedded in our everyday lives, there are also going to be more and more questions about who has the moral responsibility for the machines' actions. Ethical questions will arise that we as members of society have not had to grapple with before. For example, what if a robot in a warehouse accidentally drops a one-hundred-pound box on your foot? What happens if a robot is walking your dog, and the dog bites a neighbor's cat? Who is responsible?

Even now, questions like these are being applied to driverless vehicles, especially after an accident in Arizona where an autonomous vehicle killed a pedestrian in 2018.[46] Who was responsible for the accident? The person who wrote the software? The head of the division that made the software?

The CEO of the company? All of the above? An entirely new area of law is springing up around these questions—not to mention think tanks, research firms, and nonprofits.

Back to the Future?

Technology is not only part of the fabric of our lives, it is quite literally starting to become a part of the very fabric we wear! A team at the MIT Media Lab recently developed "smart fabrics" as part of a collection of projects that leverages the creativity and beauty inherent in "e-textiles," fabrics embedded with electronics that make possible a scarf that is also a piano keyboard! The team then used these findings to create a program that introduces middle and high schoolers to computer science.[47]

Another MIT group created a "second skin" breathable workout suit prototype that has ventilating flaps that respond to an athlete's body heat and sweat. The project, "bioLogic," includes fourteen researchers specializing in mechanical engineering, chemical engineering, architecture, biological engineering, and fashion design, as well as researchers from athletics companies.[48]

A Google X division called Project Jacquard is working with several of your favorite clothing companies, including Levi Strauss, to develop electronic clothing and denim jackets that turn a portion of the fabric on the sleeve into a touch-sensitive remote control for phones.[49] You can answer the call from your boss while riding your Onewheel, just by touching your cuff! Researchers behind the project are also investigating ways to capture biometric data such as blood pressure and pulse rate to be shared in real-time with wearers, as well as caregivers and doctors. Imagine your grandma using her sweater to send an alert to her cardiologist that her blood pressure is higher than it was yesterday!

I'm Game

The possibilities continue to blow my mind, especially regarding the virtual world. For years, virtual reality was the domain of gamers and tech enthusiasts. But today, doctors and other medical professionals use it for patient education and even as a surgical planning tool. Brain surgeons at Stanford Medicine in Palo Alto, California, can take patients on a virtual tour of their own brain before making any incision.

"We can plan out how we approach a tumor and avoid critical areas like the motor cortex or the sensory areas," says Gary Steinberg, Professor and Chair of Neurosurgery at Stanford Medicine. "Before, we did not have the ability to reconstruct it in three dimensions; we'd have to do it in our minds. This way, it's a three-dimensional rendering."[50]

Of course, this dramatically increases the likelihood of a successful surgery by providing a level of insight that did not exist previously. Not to mention answering many questions for the patient ahead of time!

Astrophysics and Hospitality

One of my favorite examples of future careers is emerging at the intersection of astrophysics and hospitality. A California-based company called Orbital Assembly is developing "Voyager Station," a space resort complete with villas and suites for rent, a gourmet restaurant, a full-service bar, and an entertainment venue. Basically, it is a "consumerized" version of the International Space Station. Guests can enjoy a luxury experience with simulated gravity and spectacular views of Earth and space.[51] (One of my first thoughts was: who is training crew members to change bed linens and mix a Martini while going around the Earth at 17,000 miles an hour? But I digress . . .)[52]

In the not-too-distant future, numerous tech and process permutations will offer unimaginable solutions driven by technology and the creative combination of unrelated disciplines. By their very nature, these solutions will generate new "careers." On the surface, the skill needs might seem daunting, but I believe anyone with a little determination can figure out them out. There are strong signals and clear indicators for how these new connections transform businesses and generate future career opportunities; you just have to watch for them and connect the dots!

Trust Your Gut

There are, of course, *many* factors that go into making career choices. Perhaps you know people working at a digital version of The Pony Express right now. Maybe you really like your current employer who is offering you a big salary bump, a prestigious title, and perhaps even stock options in the company. That is all well and good, as long as you keep in mind that a stint at the Digital Pony Express is going to be, for all intents and purposes, a short-term engagement. It will be a brief tour of duty where you might learn new skills or meet a few interesting people—maybe even potential clients or business partners for careers farther down the road. You may even encounter talented people you interact with in another setting later in your career path.

The good news? There are lots of ways and sources to help you identify what's coming next. As we've seen throughout history, innovative and exciting new careers have all been created by connecting an existing approach to a new or unlikely technology or discipline to create something new. I passionately believe that this pattern will only continue. It is certainly not new, and it is not going to stop.

By investigating historical trends (as we have in this chapter), you will start to see patterns emerge clearly. And by watching current technology trends, you can get a sense of where you might want to work, along with the opportunities to consider avoiding. Be on the alert. Be a sleuth! Look for factors creating new, successful business models and which circumstances will destroy old ones.

The only real constant is that more and more unlikely disciplines will be connecting, and the rate and pace at which they do this is only going to accelerate. We'll talk more specifically about how you can monitor these transitions in the Future Career Toolkit section of the book. The tool called ANTENNA will guide you on how to do this methodically. It only gets even more exciting from here!

– CHAPTER 7 –

Think Like a Genius

> "A human being should be able to change a diaper, plan an invasion, butcher a hog, conn a ship, design a building, write a sonnet, balance accounts, build a wall, set a bone, comfort the dying, take orders, give orders, cooperate, act alone, solve equations, analyze a new problem, pitch manure, program a computer, cook a tasty meal, fight efficiently, die gallantly. Specialization is for insects."
> —Robert A. Heinlein, Time Enough for Love (1973)

> "Talent hits a target no one else can hit.
> Genius hits a target no one else can see."
> —Arthur Schopenhauer, nineteenth-century German writer and philosopher [53]

LESSONS FOR THE NEXT GENERATION OF POLYMATHS

As described in the quotes above, I believe each of us has an innate ability to operate in multiple disciplines. People in today's fast-paced, digitally driven, mobile world are uniquely positioned to be comfortable and successful in this new climate. Sure, there are a few truly historic geniuses—da Vinci, Isaac Newton, and Benjamin Franklin, to name a few. But I believe we can *all* learn from how they approached the world—the ways in which they discovered, learned, adapted, and integrated; the strategies they used to innovate, invent, and then *reinvent* themselves. These are the kinds of skills and thinking strategies that are going to be critical for success in the twenty-first century's evolving economic and cultural models.

Renaissance Man/Woman

When someone is called a "Renaissance Man" or "Renaissance Woman" today, it implies they have broad interests or knowledge. It also suggests they have some level of accomplishment or expertise in several fields. At the very least, it means they have enough knowledge to provide an insightful, experience-driven perspective on how the larger puzzle pieces fit together, whether it's societally, culturally, scientifically, from a business perspective, or even from a historical vantage point.

This term goes back to the Renaissance (of course!) and the Age of Enlightenment, when people sought to develop skills in all areas of knowledge: science, the arts, physical development, and social accomplishments. Understanding both the arts and sciences became a highly regarded attribute. The vast majority of people of that era were not well educated, so this was an entirely new way of thinking for them.

Back then, universities did not specialize in specific areas but rather trained their students in a broad array of subjects, including science, philosophy, and theology. The idea of a universal education was pivotal—hence, "university" was the word used to describe a place where education took place. A "universal education" grounded Renaissance students broadly. From there, they could continue into apprenticeships to become Masters in a specific field.[54]

Incidentally, this is still the model in a few places like Oxford and Cambridge where students "read" in a particular subject rather than take courses that tie to more specific skills or expertise. The objective is to provide a wide range of knowledge along with the ability to see correlations across disciplines.

Polymaths in Time

Throughout human history, there have been many individuals who have had multiple talents and were able to excel across a variety of disciplines. We now refer to them as "polymaths." This comes from the Greek word meaning "having learned much," or "a person whose expertise spans a significant number of different subject areas." In less formal terms, a polymath (or polymathic person) may be someone who is very knowledgeable.[55] Most ancient scientists and philosophers were polymaths by today's standards.

In Ancient Greece, for example, there was an expectation of being well-rounded, able to perform as an athlete and as an orator. To the Greeks, the ability to play an instrument was the mark of a civilized, educated man, and through an education in all areas, it was thought that the soul could become more cultivated. In turn, Greek athletics was a channel for developing a healthy and beautiful body, which was an end in and of itself.

It is important to note that polymaths were not unique to European-based cultures. As a side note, I find it unfortunate that there is often a skewed worldview on this topic. Sure, there have been multi-talented individuals who have emerged in Western culture over thousands of years. But I would be remiss if I did not mention people from all over the globe across history, from Asia to South America, India, and Africa, who embraced skills across various disciplines. They may not have been as widely acknowledged or acclaimed as others, but their impact needs to be noted.

Shen Kuo

Shen Kuo is considered the "Chinese Leonardo da Vinci." He lived during the Song Dynasty (eleventh century), and his accomplishments include three-dimensional relief maps, modern waterworks, and other civil engineering systems. He designed a solar calendar, contributed to various advances in medicine, math, meteorology, optics, and even developed a prototype of a movable-type printer more than three hundred years before Gutenberg. He was also a poet, philosophical commentator, statesman, and military leader.[56]

Carlos de Sigüenza y Góngora

Carlos de Sigüenza y Góngora was considered one of the first great intellectuals in the New World. Born in Mexico City in 1645, he studied mathematics and astronomy under the direction of his father, a tutor for the royal family in Spain. He later became the chair of mathematics and exact sciences at the University of Mexico in 1672. He was also a poet, non-fiction writer, historian, philosopher, cartographer, and cosmographer. Such was his prestige that the French King Louis XIV himself tried to induce him to come to Paris. He wrote an almanac and, in 1693, published *El Mercurio Volante,* the first newspaper in New Spain.[57]

Hildegard of Bingen

Hildegard of Bingen was a twelfth-century German abbess. She was also a philosopher, theologian, composer, and poetess.[58] Some even say that she pioneered opera, sexology, and scientific natural history. She wrote her first book, *Scivias,* in 1141. In this book, she explained that the Earth had four elements: wind, fire, water, and earth. She also mentioned that there were different layers of air and water.[59] This was pretty remarkable insight to have in Medieval Europe, especially from a woman at the time!

Leon Battista Alberti

Leon Battista Alberti was one of the most accomplished but little-known polymaths from the Italian Renaissance. He was a humanist, author, artist, architect, poet, priest, linguist, philosopher, and cryptographer. His concepts embodied the basic tenets of Renaissance humanism: that humans were empowered and limitless in their capacities for development.[60]

Show 'Em the Old Sprezzatura

In 1478, an Italian courtier named Baldassare Castiglione wrote *The Book of the Courtier*.[61] Interestingly, Castiglione was also a diplomat and soldier, and his book addressed issues of etiquette, behavior, and morals—particularly at royal courts. He also stressed "sprezzatura," the kind of attitude that should accompany a person of many talents. He describes an ideal courtier "as having a cool mind, a good voice (with beautiful, elegant, and brave words) along with proper bearing and gestures."[62]

Not only that, Castiglione wrote that a good courtier was also expected to be an athlete, as well as have a solid knowledge of the humanities, the classics, and fine arts. A good courtier should also be able to paint, draw, and possess many other skills—always without showy or boastful behavior. He dubbed this the "sprezzatura" way of interacting with the world. You'll note that this idea is somewhat similar to the skills Robert Heinlein describes in the quote I used to start this chapter.

My Point Is...

How are the accomplishments of all of these people relevant to our discussion on how to succeed at jobs that don't exist yet? Well, these historical polymaths are known for demonstrating an openness to new ideas. Additionally, the breadth of their interests and skills spanned multiple disciplines. They can then serve as models for preparing for the twenty-first century's global borderless workplace paradigm.

All of the people I've just mentioned were each able to put together big-picture ideas that others might not have been able to see, absorb, articulate, or act on. I hope that by sharing these examples with you, you will reflect on how you yourself might think like a polymath in your everyday life. The goal is to provide a perspective around this kind of approach and encourage you to use it to navigate your own non-linear career path successfully—no matter what the setting.

I believe today's global job marketplace requires thinking like a genius. Successful workers need to understand how the world works in the early twenty-first century and have a sense of where we are in terms of a broader socio-historical context. They also need to have a broad knowledge of many disciplines.

Expertise Is Out; Mental Agility Is In

A couple of years ago, *The Atlantic* featured the article, "At Work, Expertise is Falling Out of Favor," describing the way the US Navy is staffing a new ship with hybrid sailors. These hybrid sailors are crew members who can do five or six things well in relation to the duties aboard the ship.[63]

Additionally, Laszlo Bock (former Chief People Officer at Google and now at HR start-up Humu) laid out this same approach very clearly during an interview with *The New York Times*.[64] Bock says that to work at Google, "expertise" is at the bottom of the list of eight criteria. In fact, "expertise" is listed *below* the ability to connect unlikely dots, bring new ideas to the conversation, and demonstrate emergent leadership. At Google, it's important to be able to formulate an approach to solving a problem, but you must also be willing to acquiesce if someone on the team has a better idea. More importantly, the company values the ability to figure out how your idea might support or augment your colleague's idea rather than replace it.

Much has been written about this idea: learning to look across disciplines, working outside the borders of traditional thinking and processes, being open to trying lots of different options to achieve one's objectives, facing failure without fear, learning from mistakes, and combining disciplines in new and unexpected ways. In fact, the famous Thomas Edison quote comes to mind: "I have not failed. I've just found 10,000 ways that didn't work."[65]

Thinking Like a Genius

Today's psychologists use the overarching term "cognitive disinhibition" to describe the approach that geniuses typically take.[66]

According to what I've read, two common traits associated with cognitive disinhibition are 'superfluity' and 'backtracking.'

- **Superfluity** involves generating a variety of ideas, one or more of which turn out to be useless and a complete waste of time. (I've been there; have you?)

- **Backtracking** means that the person must return to an earlier approach despite having gone off in a completely different direction. Exploring the wrong track obliges a return to options that you might have discarded originally. (Aha! Now we're talking!)

You see, venturing blindly into uncharted territory and retracing steps, backtracking, and *not being afraid of that superfluity* (seemingly 'wasted' or 'useless' activities) is a consistent attribute of many creative genius types. According to a theory proposed by psychologist Donald Campbell in 1960, creative thought emerges through a process or procedure he called blind variation and selective retention (BVSR).[67] Basically, he is saying that you have to try out ideas that might fail before hitting on a breakthrough.

I know this seems pretty obvious, but I want you to think of it in the context of navigating through a series of careers during a working lifetime. You have to engage in trial and error, or a series of "generate and test" procedures to determine the worth of an idea. In this case, it's your next career.

This way of thinking can help explain certain characteristics of extraordinarily creative minds—both now and throughout history. Openness to new ideas and varied interests leads to innovative thinking and intellectual and artistic breakthroughs. These are the kinds of skills that innovative companies and organizations will seek when hiring employees or engaging gig workers. This is what it will take for you to thrive in the business climate of the future.

So Be Leonardo on the Job!

The skills that historical polymaths exhibited can inform our behaviors here in the early twenty-first century. In today's world, there are more and more opportunities to move in multiple directions, regardless of geophysical location. Because of the increasingly broad access to information and people, we can expect more and more innovative thinking to appear in unlikely places. For example, who would have thought that a sixteen-year-old Swedish schoolgirl named Greta would take the world by storm by sharing her powerful and insightful views on the impact of climate change?

Social and mobile technologies are increasingly enabling this. Technology will continue to expand, exploiting the power of artificial intelligence and machine learning, robotics, 6G wireless networks, AR/VR, quantum information science, and other technologies we haven't even seen yet!

As you continue to read this book, I encourage you to "think like a polymath" when considering what to do in your job or what career to pursue next. Keep in mind that, in all likelihood, you will be working in numerous varied roles, perhaps in wildly different disciplines and organizations, including ones that don't exist today, over the course of your seventy-five-plus-year work life.

So, put a little "sprezzatura" into your life! It will help make you successful as you race into the constantly morphing world of work!

– CHAPTER 8 –

Overview of the Future Toolkit

If you had told me when I graduated from college that I was going to have multiple careers, I would have shaken my head and said, "What? No way!"

I always figured I would be a musician in some form or another. As it turns out, I was involved in music in different ways for over twenty years—as a performer and songwriter, and then as a jingle composer and producer. While I still play in several different bands, I have not done it for a living in over thirty years.

Admittedly, the motivating factors and the settings changed many times over the course of several decades. For example, as I described earlier, at twenty-two, I was ecstatic at the prospect of doing gigs and making records with a rock band. I was using my skills as a creative person, as a musician, performer, and composer. But then that lifestyle got old after a while, and I moved on to my next career.

As I navigated through my various roles, it seemed there were always certain traits, activities, or processes that recurred as I made these shifts. It always came down to me wanting to make a change, not being satisfied with where I was in my current career, and wanting to do something different. Always being curious. Each time, it forced me to figure out just what it was I wanted to do next, based on factors like the urge for professional growth, a need for spiritual renewal, or the experience of a sudden philosophical shift in my mindset. I would find myself wanting to do something more challenging, live a different lifestyle, increase my income, have a more stable schedule, develop a different set of friends and relationships, or even live in a different physical location. There were also influences from the outside world—changes in technology, socio-cultural trends, and political factors—that influenced my career shifts.

Seeing the big picture

Before we get into the details of the Future Career Toolkit, I want you to indulge me in a quick mental exercise. Think about this Top Ten list of phrases that were *never said* when I was in college! And dig into them to identify the broader implications each one has for related careers and skill sets that have emerged in the past fifty years. They all represent technologies that did not exist when I was in college—they have almost all been developed and applied in the past decade.

- OK, Google, set the downstairs thermostat to 65 degrees.
- Are you going to post that selfie on Instagram?
- Can I charge my cell phone somewhere?

- Does anybody know the current price of Bitcoin?
- What's the URL for the Zoom meeting?
- I just finished binge-watching my favorite show on Netflix.
- Let's call an Uber and go to the show.
- Can you PayPal me the money you owe for dinner?
- I don't know the answer; hang on, and I'll Google it.
- I am going to fire up Chat GPT to help me write that email.

Keep in mind there will be unimaginable questions tied to careers in the future such as:

- Did they complete the design for the farming environment in the spaceship headed to Mars?
- Who is delivering the additional soil to a floating wheat farm in the mid-Pacific?
- Have they replaced the drill bits at the Rare Earth Minerals mine on the asteroid Bennu?
- When will they expand the Tour Guide staff at the Marriott Luna Resort on the Moon?
- Who owns designing a new landing strip for the autonomous electric taxi fleet in New York City?

You, dear reader, will experience impactful tech-driven changes. The skills you will need to succeed across your multiple careers will be tied to tech-based advancements as equally transformative as the ones we saw in the last century. Remember this perspective as we delve into the three Future Career tools—VOICE, ANTENNA, and MESH.

Finding the Right Tools

To quote the legendary writer and ex-Harvard professor Baba Ram Dass: "If you're not doing the right thing, the universe will tell you."[68] And it did for me many times over. I'm guessing it is doing the same for you right now as you read this book. Don't let it all overwhelm you. You simply must be prepared to listen and then respond! You *also* need to have *tools* to help you take the guidance and apply it to the evolving work environment around you.

After reflecting on my career transitions so far, I have put together what I call my Future Career Toolkit based on reflecting on and then rationalizing and codifying activities associated with each career evolution. These tools represent a systematized framework that can provide guidance, both today and in the future. To develop them, I worked closely with a dear friend (ideation and creativity guru Bryan Mattimore). In fact, we have tested these techniques in numerous settings with great results!

The kit includes three tools: VOICE, ANTENNA, and MESH. In the chapters that follow, I describe each tool and provide activities and exercises that you can use to successfully navigate your multimodal career.

Here's what to expect:

Chapter 9: Finding Your Unique VOICE

Your first step is clarifying your VOICE, or your "personal brand," in the job marketplace. I think of this as a human product development exercise at its core. In fact, in the twenty-first-century's global workplace environment, having your own unique voice and expressing it clearly and consistently is critically important. And it starts at an early age, like it or not.

The VOICE tool is designed to help you discover what you do well and what you could leverage in a series of career/job settings to navigate the new global workplace paradigm we've discussed in this book.

It is worth noting that the VOICE exercise is designed not just to point you to a private sector role. You may discover that your interests lie in other settings, such as government, a non-profit, an NGO, or a volunteer setting.

I use an ideation technique that uses your affinity for certain books, movies, TV shows, or games as triggers to discover your specific personality characteristics and proclivities. These findings represent the core input for the next two tools.

Chapter 10: Fine Tuning Your ANTENNA

The ANTENNA exercise is designed to help you find sources where conversations tied to your VOICE attributes are being conducted. You'll want to find discussions via digital media, traditional channels, and live events that are laying the foundation for the next generation of business models. In turn, this will lead to new products and services, which will translate to future career opportunities.

The ANTENNA tool also shows you how to build a table that uses the VOICE exercise as the starting point. Then, you'll learn to find sources—from newspapers and blogs to YouTube channels, TikTok videos, and Instagram influencers. The other key aspect of this tool is assigning a rhythm for how often you check them for updated content and insight.

Keep in mind that these ANTENNA sources will morph, change, and evolve over the course of your multimodal career path. But it is important to learn this technique now with the understanding that it only reflects a "point in time" view of where you want to be listening and learning at present.

Chapter 11: MESH with the Right People

The third tool, MESH, is designed to address the old adage typically associated with careers in show business: "It's not what you know, but who you know." Today, this is critical to success in every business!

I like to think of it as a visualization of your expanding network. The objective is to find specific people and communities leading conversations on the topics you are interested in. This allows you to connect with them so that you can participate in new work models and position yourself for your next career.

Make building your network your second job and create a routine! If you get to the end of the week and you have not added five people to your LinkedIn network, get to it. Put down the gaming console, turn off Netflix, make yourself another cup of coffee, and start connecting!

Do some research and find people who can help you. Simply put, at the end of the day, it is a numbers game. The more people who know who you are, the better your odds of landing your next exciting career . . . and the one(s) after that.

Let's go! You are now on your way to finding your next career!

– CHAPTER 9 –

Where Do You Stand Out? "VOICE"

> "To be yourself in a world that is constantly trying to make you something else is the greatest accomplishment."
> —Ralph Waldo Emerson[69]

FINDING YOUR UNIQUE VOICE

Everyone comes into this world wired in a certain way. Don't get me wrong: I know that environment and education *certainly* play important roles. But I also believe that the real key to lifelong success is figuring out 1) where your natural talents lie and then 2) focusing on them to achieve career success.

It sounds pretty simple, right? But this is, in fact, a crucial assessment you need to make in order to advance your career—no matter what those careers might be.

A Range of Skills

I remember years ago being at a parent event at our son's school. A psychologist was talking to a group of us about what kinds of skills and talents our kids may have, along with how we might support them. To set the overall tone, she said to the group, "OK, everyone who does *everything well, raise your hand!*"

Of course, no one did. Her point was that we each have certain talents and gifts and proclivities. And that it is perfectly OK. That's how we stand out and make an impact on the world around us. The same principle applies to careers. To progress on a career journey, you need to first understand *who you are.* Then, what is it that makes you stand out as unique? What are the things that you do that make you, *you?* What are the things that you do *well?*

Lionel Robbins, the legendary British economist who taught at the London School of Economics for over thirty years, famously said, "It really is true that if all the best tutors in the world were to concentrate on most people, they couldn't produce an Einstein, they couldn't produce a Mozart."

In other words, what combination of skills and experience do *you* bring to the planet? To your everyday interactions? To the global workforce marketplace eager to hire new talent? In the increasingly borderless work environment, identifying and promoting your own unique and specific talents is more important than ever before. Think of it as finding and devising your own personal brand, or VOICE.

Finding Your Unique "VOICE"

I have used the word VOICE, based on my extensive experience in the music business. In that industry, each person's unique approach is described as their VOICE, regardless of whether they are a singer, instrumentalist, composer, or arranger. For musicians, VOICE is a combination of things: the way they phrase, their actual sound, the way they create a groove, or their presence on stage or in the studio. And it can be so much more!

I remember once I was sitting in a recording studio in New York City with legendary saxophone player Michael Brecker. As we listened to a solo he had just recorded, Michael explained to me how the musical content in each part reflected his various musical influences. As we enjoyed the playback of his solo, he cocked his head thoughtfully when I asked him about his inspirations. Then, as a particular moment in the solo played over the speakers, he said, "Those are my John Coltrane-inspired licks," referencing the famous jazz tenor sax player.

After another few seconds, he said, "That phrasing is based on my analysis of Sam Rivers's approach," he mused, referencing yet another jazz great. "I love how he plays at the edges of what is allowed in traditional harmony."

A few moments later, Michael turned to me and grinned as a unique musical sound filled the room. "And that? That is what I can do that nobody else can do!"

Over his career, Michael developed a totally unique way of performing that created a magical, intense, and personal effect. In other words, he had found his own unique VOICE.

Based on this experience, VOICE is the perfect metaphor for the unique way we all represent ourselves in the world and in our careers.

Your VOICE in *Today's* World

Changes in business models are driving the need for a clear VOICE from people like you today, as we've discussed in this book. Learning how to create, define, develop, and morph *your* VOICE is not a matter of ego stroking or simply an activity that would be fun to do if you had the time. It is a mission-critical task that every worker today needs to take on regardless of age if they want to be successful in the twenty-first century's workplace.

Remember: in today's world, we are shifting more and more toward "the gig economy," where specialists take on assignments from various entities rather than working solely for one company. This can put you at an advantage AND disadvantage all at once. People all over the world are going to be working *with you* as well as competing *against you* in a globally connected workforce. This is yet another reason why you need to focus on defining and promoting your personal VOICE: identifying and featuring what you do that no one else can do is key to finding your next career.

Changes Are Coming

Future work environments will certainly use virtual spaces to share ideas and create work products. Collaboration will be achieved through video, virtual reality, and, eventually, even holographic projections. Think about receiving input and resources from contributors all over the planet and beyond! It would be today's telepresence on steroids. In fact, you may want to brace yourself for your grandchildren someday staring at you in disbelief: "You mean you *actually* had to physically go somewhere to do your job, and then you had to sit there all day?! In *one spot?!*"

All that to say this: *individual* contributors must have a strong, clearly represented VOICE to be successful in the new world of work. Not having a strong VOICE could be a dealbreaker! And once your VOICE is clearly established, word will spread about what YOU can do that no one else can. And you will get an exciting job!

And just like the music business, when opportunities come up, people will recommend someone they know and have worked with. For example, in music, a drummer might be asked which bass player they like to work with. Or you could ask a sax player to assemble a horn section based on trumpet players and trombone players they know.

Now, think about making that same method work for YOU in the future workplace model. The stronger and more clearly represented your VOICE is, the better your odds of landing on the next project . . . and the next . . . and the next . . .

And it can all start right now.

The Process of Finding Your VOICE TODAY

As I said, more and more organizations are already building teams with different talents and VOICES, and we are already seeing indicators that this approach is a winning model. In fact, MIT's Media Lab has been doing this for years.[70] In any given workgroup, you might have a physicist, an ethnographer, a graphic designer, a coder, a sociologist, and a mechanical engineer. Together, they share ideas, build solutions, and create innovative results.

And I cannot say this enough: YOU need to be ready for these market opportunities!

If you take a step back and think about it from a historical perspective, major thinkers and contributors to culture and society for thousands of years have had what could be termed their brand or VOICE: Leonardo da Vinci. Julius Caesar. Benjamin Franklin. Queen Victoria. Aristotle. Shakespeare. Cleopatra. Einstein. Roosevelt. Martin Luther King Jr., Nelson Mandela, John F. Kennedy, and Steve Jobs. The list goes on and on.

Each of these people had/has a clearly defined voice and uses (d) it to inspire followers, defend against enemies and naysayers, wield influence, and change culture and society. Their personal brands live on. Some used clay tablets, others created content with a quill pen, and still others recorded their thoughts in books or more modern media like radio, TV, film, and a variety of social media channels.

Today's tools of blogs, websites, and social media help us achieve the same objectives: the sharing of ideas, demonstrating expertise, increasing personal influence, and thus establishing our VOICE. Today, it is the age of instant communication, online transparency in our daily lives, and constant digital interaction and collaboration. In a way, everyone already builds and monitors their VOICE. But it may not happen the way that you think.

You Are What You Post

I remember once after a workshop, a high school student asked me if I thought he had a VOICE, even though he hadn't started his career yet. I countered, "Are you on X/Twitter? Instagram? Do you text your friends? Do you wear clothing with logos on it?" The answer, of course, was "Yes."

Any place your perspective and worldview are represented on X/Twitter, Instagram, Pinterest, Facebook, LinkedIn, or TikTok establishes and represents your VOICE through photos, videos, comments, or "likes." It has the same impact as if you were doing a presentation in a class or speaking up in a meeting: you are presenting your VOICE to others. Your VOICE is part of every interaction you have with the world both on and offline.

The VOICE Exercise

To differentiate yourself in this era of the planet-wide, talented workforce all using the same social media platforms to connect with others, you have to focus on your own personal VOICE relentlessly. A clearly articulated VOICE lets people, companies, team leaders, and colleagues understand who you are and why they should maybe hire you. This will be critically important in order to stay "employable."

That's why I came up with the VOICE Exercise. This exercise uses an "ideation technique" as a way to come up with lots of ideas for addressing an issue in a judgment-free brainstorming session. Essentially, the exercise uses your personal preferences to help you identify topics you think are valuable and perspectives that resonate with you. This also helps you identify where you have skills and interests.

By uncovering areas of interest and passion, you can more easily decide where to focus your efforts in terms of what specific industry or type of organization you might want to work for with that unique VOICE of yours. This exercise can also help you identify *additional skills you might need to be successful in your next career.*

STEP 1: Identify Positive "Triggers"

Start by thinking of a movie, book, TV show, or video, or board game that you love. Better yet, select more than one, just as long as your picks really resonate with you. Your choices could include a movie you saw recently or a TV show you loved from your childhood. It could be a game you played in middle school or a book you read last year on vacation.

Next, think about why your choices affect you. What aspect of each one spoke to you and might have influenced you? The reasons might be from your childhood or even your recent experiences, but the idea is that your choices will help you recognize your interests and talents.

Don't overthink it. Just write down what comes to mind.

FAVORITE	TOPIC

STEP 2: Tease Out the Characteristics

Once you have identified your positive triggers, reflect on the two or three aspects of each one that made you select it.

Questions to ask yourself:

- Are there characteristics of the characters or plot that resonate with me? Or is it the costumes or set design that moved me?
- Was it the pace of gameplay, weapons choices, or avatar options? Were there certain aspects that just made me feel centered? Excited? Empowered?
- What do I like about it? What struck a chord with me? What was it about that trigger that really made me feel great or inspired or motivated?

Maybe you liked the movie *Star Wars: The Rise of Skywalker*. Perhaps it was the use of futuristic technology or the sense of teamwork and camaraderie among a diverse group of people and creatures. Or, more broadly, maybe the focus on hope and the possibilities of overcoming fear drew you in.

Take your time with this exercise. You are simply looking for themes and key aspects of your personality and skill set.

STEP 3: Capture the Insight

Now, I want you to create a table to capture these positive triggers and the qualities they represent.

Let me give you an example of how this works for me. I chose *Blade Runner 2049* as one of my favorite movies. As you can probably tell by now, I am fascinated by future technology and its implications for business and culture and society. In particular, I am fascinated by the way the movie represented robots and the cyborg-like transhumanist possibilities that were explored.

I also picked a book called *"MORE: A History of the World Economy from the Iron Age to the Information Age."* The author is a well-known writer at The Economist, Philip Coggan. At the end of the day, all careers are based at a meta-level on business. I find it fascinating, although sometimes my eyes glaze over when they get into too much numerical detail or cross-referencing of other economists' research. But the way economies and businesses and organizations have evolved are clear indicators of jobs and careers.

Here is an example of what my VOICE table might look like.

FAVORITE	TOPIC
MOVIE - Blade Runner 2049	Future culture, technology
BOOK - MORE: The World Economy from the Iron Age to the Information Age-Philip Coggin	Economics, global business

STEP 4: Put It into Action

Once you have teased out the reasons why your selected positive "triggers" resonate with you, take a hard look at your list. Think about how these key aspects might have been part of your life for a long time and could continue to be part of your life in the future.

In my case, I sense that I will continue to be interested in future tech, business, and culture and, as a result, continue to work in roles where this interest is rewarded. I see myself writing, speaking, designing, and conducting workshops around these general topics for at least the foreseeable future.

Now What?

In summary, the VOICE exercise allows you, dear reader, to determine what your primary (or perhaps even subliminal!) areas of interest are in order to identify where to focus your career, both now and in the future.

And this works!

I have used the VOICE exercise in numerous workshops in various settings, from university classrooms to seventh-grade career day fairs to sessions advising senior executives. I have found it to be very effective in ferreting out topics of interest that you may not have been able to identify in any other way.

Why not give it a try? It is a risk-free and enlightening exercise that you can do regardless of whether you are searching for a new career or not. You can use the VOICE exercise to help understand your current areas of focus and interest and identify how your interests might have shifted—because they will certainly change throughout your life.

As you know by now, my voice has morphed and evolved at least eight times throughout my career, from being a touring rock musician to writing jingles for TV commercials to managing social media for a global technology company. So, keep in mind that your voice is going to shift and evolve as well. You need to stay in touch with it and use it to navigate your own career journey.

– CHAPTER 10 –

Fine-Tuning Your Info-Gathering "ANTENNA"

> "Five Exabytes of information were created between the dawn of civilization through 2003, but that much information is now created every two days, and the pace is increasing!"
> —Eric Schmidt, Google CEO, 2010[71]

> "You're gonna need a bigger boat."
> —Chief Brody, Jaws, 1975

Congratulations! You have now identified your VOICE: the things that make you, *you*; the vision that drives you, excites you, and motivates you. Those qualities that are essentially the core of your personal brand that will bring you success in the job marketplace. Next, let's take all of that and apply it to the next Future Career Tool: I call it Fine-Tuning Your ANTENNA.

The overarching objective of the ANTENNA tool is to identify and monitor conversations around topics from the VOICE exercise that interest you. Basically, you want to find where today's innovative and passionate people are writing, speaking, publishing, sharing, and meeting about the things you are passionate about. These locations will be where new business models are evolving. And because of that, they are also where future careers are being born.

The key? Find specific content that is related to your current topics of interest. That's the essence of the ANTENNA exercise.

The *good* news is that there are *lots* of valuable and easily accessible resources available in today's world. The *bad* news is that there are *lots* of valuable and easily accessible resources available in today's world. The key is learning to perform information triage.

Information Comes in Many Forms

I remember having an epiphany at the British Museum in London a few years ago. It was a moment that got me thinking about the ongoing evolution of the ways in which information is captured and transmitted. I found myself staring at the Library of Ashurbanipal. It's a collection of over thirty thousand clay tablets and fragments created by an Assyrian king in the seventh century B.C. They are inscribed with cuneiform (a type of writing used in Mesopotamia or ancient Iraq). Translating the words on these tablets essentially allows modern-day humans to travel back in time to follow palace court intrigues, listen in on secret intelligence reports, and learn about various religious rituals and ceremonies step-by-step. Through the collection, we can almost hear the words of songs and prayers being uttered; we can thumb through medical handbooks and read about the deeds of the king and his court in incredible detail.

As I stared at the display in front of me, I wondered: A thousand years from now, what will future historians call a modern collection of today's Tweets, TikTok videos, Instagram posts, and blogs? Will the people of tomorrow be able to track our daily lives by the posts we leave behind? Will they even understand it?

The ways in which data and insight are created and shared are constantly changing, whether thousands of years ago or even ten years ago. The tactics and channels for content delivery are morphing and even disappearing altogether once humans move on from them. Just think of Ask Jeeves, MySpace, Friendster, and AOL.

What is the message I want you to take away from my musings about changing technology? **Never limit yourself.** Always consider and track down any potential sources of information or insight, however unlikely they may seem. In the next chapter, we'll talk about the MESH exercise where we will narrow down the actual people and organizations leading the way on forward-thinking conversations about business and culture. These are the people who are creating the next generation of careers: yours *and mine!*

Dealing with Information Overload

The current flood of information spewed out every second of every day represents an overwhelming volume of data to scour and use. There is no way around that fact. In fact, writer Dhruba Karki stated that as of November 2020, over 2.5 *quintillion* bytes of data were being created every day, and that number was only increasing. Amazingly, over 90 percent of this has been created within just the past five years![72]

Learning how to identify and filter information sources will be the key to your success when using the ANTENNA tool because the tsunami of data continues to increase every day. Millions of resources provide information on topics related to the workplace of the future: newspapers, magazines, websites, Wikipedia entries, TV programs, TED Talks, blogs, YouTube videos, Instagram, Pinterest, X/Twitter, TikTok, Clubhouse, Bluesky, RedNote, and on and on. And more channels of information are certainly coming online every day. While the information overload can be a little nerve-wracking, the upside is that it gives you many options, which is empowering!

Where to Start

My recommendation is to start with macro-level content providers that deliver a big-picture perspective. Examples might include elite newspapers, like *The New York Times, Wall Street Journal*, and *The Washington Post*. While they still use dead trees to deliver content, they also have apps and websites. Select whichever delivery mode you are comfortable with. They all publish a variety of topic-specific newsletters as well.

You might start each day by taking a look at one (or all!) of these newspapers in order to be up to date on what's going on in the world of your interest. (My preferred starting point is typically *The New York Times* because I lived in Manhattan for sixteen years . . . but to each his own.).

Also keep in mind you want to have a global "big picture" perspective to ground you and inform your more in-depth searches. Remember that we are global citizens and part of a much larger community than our hometown or even our home country.

Once you have gotten yourself oriented to the larger perspective, drill down deeper to get more specifics using criteria such as a particular discipline, a geographical location, or any other qualifier that might help you figure out what your next move might be. Then collect as much data in your area of expertise or interest as you can find. Track down what is happening in specific fields you are interested in. Look for trends in whatever topic makes your heart beat a bit faster with excitement. The sky is the limit.

Look at the details

Your next step is to zoom in and get more specific. Again, there are many resources and channels out there to help you. For example, I have several Google Alerts set up to monitor various trends I am interested in (artificial intelligence, robotics, and quantum information science, for example). I let Google do the work of scouring the Web to find content I am interested in based on my specific criteria at any given point in time.

One of my personal favorite sources is the *MIT Technology Review*. They're always very up-to-date on interesting stuff from university labs, as well as how innovative solutions are being applied in the business world. You can also use sites like UpContent that search and collect information around criteria you define. This tool builds a dashboard that lets you quickly scan and even distribute relevant content to others. I use this tool primarily for my X/Twitter feed to share new and pertinent material I find.

Unique cultural strategy agencies like Sparks & Honey are devoted to trend-spotting. They also live stream their daily review sessions on Facebook, providing tremendous insight into what's happening from a cultural perspective on a global scale within the past twenty-four to forty-eight hours.

Bloomberg Businessweek is a weekly magazine that provides insights into business and technology. It's a great resource focused on business that's written in a user-friendly tone yet still gives readers a wealth of valuable information. They also have an app that is easy to navigate and is updated frequently.

All that to say this: there are resources out there for you to find out more about the topics and trends that excite you!

Follow the Money

Remember to investigate trends in funding and investment. Research entrepreneur and investor terminology like "angels" and "private equity." Find out which start-ups investors believe are worth putting their money into. Some of these ventures will actually emerge to become the next innovative companies doing interesting stuff in the marketplace. As a result, they will need people with new skills to drive their business model.

The key reason for all of this research is that it provides invaluable insight into *emerging* business models. It can also give you an indicator of the kinds of skills that are going to be needed in emerging fields and what you, as a potential employee or contractor, will need to be a part of their workforce.

Other resources for tuning your ANTENNA to what is trending in business include The Silicon Valley Business Journal (news about which startups were funded and where there are changes in executive personnel or mergers and acquisitions), CBinsights.com (research on investments and economic indicators), and angellist.com (a blog with information on where deals are being made and what companies are obtaining funding and why).

Find the Right People

To keep your ANTENNA tweaked, you need to be aware of people producing interesting events about the future business space. Google Tim O'Reilly and add him to your list. He is a publisher and event producer who conducts very enlightening conferences, usually in San Francisco and New York. He also publishes a newsletter, and his website even has a section on "Insights, tools and strategies for building twenty-first-century businesses." Great stuff.

Keynote speakers and panels at various conferences and trade events are populated with executives and thought leaders representing all kinds of different perspectives: business leaders, investors, academics, and think tank researchers. The conversations at these events are designed to cover all kinds of trends in the context of economic and cultural impact. They also often discuss business models and prospects for value creation in the near term and long term. All of this comes with implications for skill needs and career paths.

Another source of insight into cultural and business trends is The Institute for the Future. One of the leading players in foresight and future strategy development, IFTF is based in Silicon Valley near Stanford University. They publish numerous reports on a range of topics, including health, education, food, and transportation. They also run in-person workshops. Much of their research is available for free on their website.

Additionally, check out Ray Kurzweil. He's one of the founders of Singularity University and has written extensively about the future. He is probably best known for his theories regarding computers becoming sentient beings—the "singularity"—and he writes extensively on what he sees as an inevitable outcome: when computers, thanks to artificial intelligence and machine learning, will have emotions and can interact with us. Talk about envisioning the future!

Like, Follow, Favorite, DM

Of course, social media channels should factor into the ANTENNA resources you gather. Set up a designated

X/Twitter account to follow thought leaders and various organizations. All of the sources, publishers, and channels I mentioned before have numerous X/Twitter accounts and publish new information regularly.

I tend not to use Facebook very much, which is owned by the company Meta. But you probably know as well as I do that many people use it in very impactful ways. As with anything, you just have to do some research to find the right thought leaders that align with your areas of interest, then set notifications to alert you the next time they post new content so that it shows up in your newsfeed. You may even research ways to use the site to connect with almost three billion users. The sheer size of that potential audience certainly makes it worth investigating, even if it's not the #1 social media site for many age groups, anymore.

I find sites like Medium.com very interesting in general and also more valuable in terms of career development and management. You can search with tags like "Future of Work," for example, and it pulls up some remarkably interesting articles.

Numerous other social media channels can provide rich content and insight. YouTube, of course, offers a variety of resources on every subject imaginable. One of my favorites is a video called *"Did You Know."* The animated video lays out stats about what's trending in global education, business, social media adoption, and many other topics. Best of all, the video is updated annually. Another video is called *"Shift Happens."* It's also updated about once a year and contains insight into global meta trends.

Don't Forget LinkedIn

Most job seekers know that one of the most important online tools today is LinkedIn. While this is typically thought of as a place to post your resume or CV, it also provides a very active and growing publishing platform. LinkedIn's stated mission is "to connect talent with opportunity on a global scale as well as provide access to learning content," which is why they bought the online training company Lynda.com in 2015. They were then purchased by Microsoft in 2016, They clearly understand the connection between skills and employability and are looking to drive new models.

LinkedIn provides not only a forum for people to share background information in their profiles but also allows users to establish their expertise by publishing posts and commenting in communities. Additionally, LinkedIn Learning has a vast library of curriculum designed to help users address skills gaps. These can also be used to help you navigate multiple roles throughout a lifelong career trajectory.

As a side note, it goes without saying that to get the most out of the site, you need to have a robust profile on LinkedIn. I also suggest signing up for a Premium account. First, a badge appears on your main page and shows the world that you understand the value of this tool. Second, it lets you send direct messages to people you do not know, digital cold calls called "InMails." I have used this capability many times to track down people with expertise in a specific topic or to ask for help connecting with people I have not met.

You Can't Know Where You're Going Until You Know Where You've Been

It might sound cliche, but it's true: we can get a clearer picture of what's coming by looking at what has been. So, I also recommend reading books and other resources about the history of economics and technology to get perspective on how we got to today's world.

I've already mentioned one of my favorites called *Technological Revolutions and Financial Capital* by Carlota Perez, a Venezuelan economist and professor at the London School of Economics. You may want to check out other related books: *A History of the World Economy from the Iron Age to the Information Age* by Philip Coggan (from my VOICE exercise) and *The Classical School: The Birth of Economics in 20 Enlightened Lives* by Callum Williams. There are many others, but these are two great resources to get you started.

The ANTENNA Exercise

All of what I just described—from books and magazines to apps and Tweets—is designed to provide ideas about where you might find the kinds of conversations that connect your VOICE to people, companies, and organizations in the real world.

The ANTENNA exercise provides a codified process for collecting and analyzing knowledge that will benefit you. It provides guidance for identifying the skills needed for your next career and ideas for how and where to acquire them. Essentially, it is an exercise designed to help you identify where future careers that align with your interests are emerging and where you can leverage your skills. So, let us look at each step of ANTENNA.

STEP 1: Cast a Wide Net

The process starts by looking for information sources based on what interests you or areas that excite you, all based on the previous VOICE exercise. While finding appropriate sources may seem daunting, you've already done some of this work already—whether you realize it or not!

Start by:
- Scanning your inboxes. Look for any newsletters you already subscribe to that connect to topics from the VOICE exercise.
- Make a list of the apps on your phone that provide the content you are drawn to.
- Check out websites that you have stored in your browser's bookmarks.
- Revisit newspapers or magazines that you read regularly or a blog whose author and topics resonate with you.

See? You have already made many important decisions about content that interests you! The ANTENNA tool will simply help you think about them in a much more programmed and formal way. Remember that you are essentially looking for economic activity, business models, innovative technologies, new processes and approaches, inventions, and partnerships, all happening just outside of *current* economic and cultural norms. Many are heading toward the mainstream, where they will foster innovation and influence transitions in business and society. In turn, these changes translate into new career opportunities.

You also need to be ready for "random encounters with knowledge." Be open to finding new sources in unexpected, serendipitous ways that will add insights to enrich your career exploration experience.

Simply put, you want to find sources of insight where forward-thinking, passionate, smart, thoughtful people share perspectives and concepts that align with the VOICE topics you have identified. The challenge becomes prioritization, determining which ones to select and focus on. Believe me, I still struggle with this myself!

STEP 2: Narrow the List Down

At the end of the day, after you identify numerous sources based on your areas of expertise and find trends in whatever topics excite you, you will need to shorten and focus the list. Do some radical triage on your source material.

Read through all of the options and pick the ones you like based on whether the content seems interesting, is presented in a compelling way, seems relevant, and/or is easy to consume and understand. Pick sources you are comfortable with. That's it. Just pick a few you like and begin!

Also, keep in mind that these sources will change as your career path develops. Back in my bass player days, I read the British pop music newspaper, *New Musical Express.* Then, I switched to *MacWorld* magazine as I transitioned to being a web producer. Nowadays, I read *The Economist* to stay on top of the latest trends in global business and newsletters from

The Quantum Insider. This mapping is a living document that will change as your career path does.

STEP 3: Build a Grid of Sources and Establish a Protocol

The next step is to organize the sources you have identified as well as how frequently you are going to monitor them.

The ANTENNA grid consists of four columns. Here is what it looks like:

VOICE ATTRIBUTE	SOURCE	DESCRIPTION	FREQUENCY

- Take the VOICE attributes you discovered in the previous chapter and list them in the left-most column of the grid.
- In the second column, put the name of the source, like The New York Times or Instagram.
- In the third column, enter a description of the source. Is it a website? A magazine? An app? Jot down if it's a blog or social media account. Perhaps it's a YouTube channel or even a group on LinkedIn. Maybe it's something else entirely.
- Finally, in the fourth column, determine just how often you might check each source. You can base this on factors like how often they publish new content or how closely it aligns with your VOICE attributes.
- Here is an example of my own current ANTENNA grid based on the VOICE criteria I teased out: Future Culture, Tech, and Global Business. I have also called out how frequently I access these sources.

VOICE ATTRIBUTE	SOURCE	DESCRIPTION	FREQUENCY
Future culture	Futurism	Newsletter, Web site	Daily
	The Futures Agency	Webinars	Periodically
Tech	Silicon Valley Business Journal	Print newspaper	Weekly
	BBC Click	YouTube, Twitter	Weekly, twice a day
Global business	Bloomberg Tech	TV show	Weekly
	Espresso (Economist)	App	Twice daily

Again, the idea is to establish a routine where you are continually looking at sources of information that keep you curious and pique your interests as they evolve. This will help you shape what your next career exploration might be and where to turn for more information, including what new skills you might need to get into a new role.

Additional Tip: Keep a "New Job Journal"

Once you have created your ANTENNA grid, create a designated notebook, Word doc, or note on your phone. Try using an app like Pocket or Evernote where you can:

- Capture the *two to three most interesting articles* or data points you uncovered at the end of each week.
- Jot down the sources and a summary of the content. Collect and store this data so you can later analyze it more thoroughly.
- Identify and list the synergies emerging between the sources that could be early signs of a new career opportunity.
- Pick a day of the week for this process. Maybe every Friday at 6 p.m.? Perhaps the first Monday of the month at lunchtime. Or the last Sunday of the month. Do whatever works with your schedule, but make sure you assign a date for your review and stick to it.

Incidentally, it might surprise you to learn that this kind of grid-based notetaking and analysis has been used by any number of influential people throughout history. In fact, this exercise was inspired by one of my favorite polymaths, Benjamin Franklin. Franklin created a somewhat similar matrix to monitor his own behavior against a set of moral criteria he had defined. He called his grid "The Thirteen Virtues."[73]

Once you have made this list and reviewed it, see what patterns emerge. What future jobs or careers are implied by analyzing this data? What unlikely disciplines look like they might be moving toward intersection? What is it about a particular data point that piqued your interest? How might you contribute to this new way of doing business with your unique skillset? How could you get involved? More importantly, what current skills do you have that you could leverage? What additional skills would you have to learn?

Are there implications in your findings for a future job now? Eight months from now? Eight years from now? Do you see other people also starting to connect dots in new ways among the disciplines you are interested in? Do you see a gap that might be filled, a possible job or career that could be created around two or three or more disciplines?

These kinds of information sources will give you the data you will need to make smart, strategic decisions about what your role might be and where you could contribute. Using this insight and analysis will lay the groundwork for helping you figure out what your next amazing career is going to be.

Analyzing the ANTENNA Results to Find Your Next Career

I want to share a technique I have developed to help you connect the dots in your career search to further take advantage of the ANTENNA tool.

The objective is to give you an additional process to help accelerate identifying possible future career opportunities by examining content—a news article, a blog, a white paper, a TikTok video–whatever the source. This technique is channel and media delivery method agnostic.

Here is how it works:

Take one of the content sources you found in the ANTENNA exercise. Don't limit yourself. Use elite newspapers. TikTok videos, TED Talks. Websites. TV shows. Blogs. Tweets. Clubhouse events. In-person conferences. X (X/

Twitter). Finding the right sources and managing how you interact with their content is the challenge.

Do a Google search and find three to five media outlets or content providers that will help you continue to focus your attention on the areas that are of most interest to you and where you might be able to leverage existing skills, experience, and relationships as well as areas where you don't have skills and would need to learn. Or where you don't know any or many people in that space but one that looks interesting or fascinating and is an area you might be interested in navigating to for your next career.

Some sources of future business-oriented content that I suggest include:

- *BBC Click* (TV show).
- Futurism (website).
- Bloomberg Studio 1.0: interviews with Silicon Valley execs (TV show).
- MIT Tech Review (website, newsletters).
- Wall Street Journal.
- The Quantum Insider (website, newsletters).
- TechCrunch (website).
- The Economist (website, magazine).

Another content source I leverage to identify future careers is *The Silicon Valley Business Journal.* Published in San Francico, the content is focused on technology funding activity as well as real estate transactions and other business news from the South Bay and San Francisco area. A recent post on a web page that is called The Funded listed twelve Bay Area startups who had raised a total of nearly $300M.

This means they have money to spend, and the implications are for increasing headcount = hiring = career opportunities.

To get a sense of which content creators and thought leaders to follow, find an interesting story and look at the elements that make it up and see what areas align with your interests and what skills you might have or need and what the implications are for a future job.

Here is how it might work.

First, set up a series of Google Alerts around the topics you teased out in your VOICE exercise. Keep in mind that they will vary and morph and change as you throughout your work life.

Mine have evolved over the years but as of this writing, my areas of interest include topics such as the metaverse, quantum, crypto, and fintech. Content appears in my inbox as emails with around three to five news articles that the Google spider has culled from crawling across the Internet looking for related content based on my alert criteria. To do this, go to alerts.google.com. It is very easy, and it is free!

Google will then send you individual emails for each topic area that you have selected, but you can also choose to have it create a Daily Digest that aggregates the content it is collecting. Like anything in today's world of the data tsunami, managing the flow and doing triage on the incoming is challenging but also gives you myriad options for learning and exploring.

Ideally, read these articles every day. I often skim the selections presented, looking for topics of interest based on my VOICE criteria. Some, of course, are more relevant than others. The tool is hardly perfect at pulling relevant content, but it shortens the cycle time to finding valuable, preselected information, and for that, we are deeply indebted to Google.

Digging into the Details

This approach will give you a starting point that ties the VOICE and ANTENNA exercises together nicely. But let's dig down into the information we have found to see how it reveals possible future career opportunities. I pulled this random example from one of my recent alerts.

Look for headlines in news stories or blogs or TV shows or YouTube/TikTok videos that make you ask the question, "What are they talking about? How will that work? Who came up with that concept?"

Here is the headline that got my attention. It is from a website called Cointelegraph.

EXAMPLE #1: Island Nation Turns to Metaverse to Preserve Its Disappearing Heritage

The subheading is this: The island of Tuvalu said it plans to build a digital version of itself in order to preserve its history as it faces erasure due to climate change.[74]

That's a new set of careers for several people!

The backstory is that in late 2022, the country's foreign minister, Simon Kofe, told the COP27 climate summit that he is trying to figure out alternative ways to protect the country's heritage against rising sea levels brought on by climate change. One of those ways is through recreating itself in the metaverse. In a video broadcast, he said, "As our land disappears, we have no choice but to become the world's first digital nation." Currently, around 40 percent of the nation's capital district is underwater at high tide and the entire country is forecast to be underwater by the end of the century. Scary!

As Tuvalu builds itself into the metaverse, it will become the first digitized nation in the metaverse. Kofe said the country's land, ocean, and culture are its most precious assets, and no matter what happens in the physical world, they will be kept safe in the cloud:

"Islands like this one won't survive rapid temperature increases, rising sea levels, and droughts, so we will recreate them virtually."

Although Tuvalu could become the first sovereign nation to recreate itself in the metaverse, other countries have already begun exploring the digital frontier. When viewed through the cross-disciplinary career lens, this article implies many exciting options.

If this initiative doesn't represent a treasure trove of cross-disciplinary career implications, I don't know what does.

When I read this, I saw five clearly implied career opportunities. They are going to have to build a team with people who have skills and interest in these areas:

1. Metaverse developer.
2. Environmental scientist.
3. Public policy/government wonk.
4. Historian to make sure the right stuff gets preserved.

5. Artistic director.

Let's drill down into the skill needs and by inference possible future-oriented career paths that this article is calling out . . .

1. Metaverse developer

This one is the most obvious. This tiny island nation will have to hire someone who develops real-looking VR environments in order to create their vision of a digital version of the country. Think if it as a sort of a digital twin. The vendor will be a company with skills in recreating real-world environments in VR. Possible suppliers might include companies like Virbela, ENGAGE, Spatial, FRAME—maybe even Meta. The market is certainly going to cover a range of developers, perhaps from game-oriented environments like Roblox, World of Warcraft, Call of Duty, Fortnight or Decentraland, as well as companies that develop more real-world settings like Virbela or even Second Life. How it is created, preserved, and/or modified will be critical as the impact of climate change continues to wreak havoc on the island.

2. Environmental scientist

Someone who is familiar with the implications of climate change on real estate and land and ideally understands the impact on island environments will be key to developing this solution. But that person must also be familiar with metaverse and XR environments. Tuvalu will need to hire a person who is passionate about their island culture and also has a broader global perspective on how climate change is impacting every country, not just island nations that are dealing with sea level rise.

3. **Public policy and regulatory skills**

   A team member who has experience navigating policy processes from a government perspective will be required. How do you set up a bid for this kind of work? Who gets selected? How do you define a budget and bid it out? What constitutes a viable project plan, and how does it align with other priorities competing for funding? Other pet projects are certainly vying for limited funding allocated to other public sector needs like infrastructure, education, healthcare, housing, etc.

4. **Historian, ethnographer, sociologist**

   A resource will have to be engaged who understands native cultures and how to interact with purveyors of traditions in native or indigenous populations, particularly people living on a remote island! He or she will have to determine what is, in fact, important to preserve and what can be discarded. Interacting with the purveyors of the culture to make specific choices about where to focus and what to preserve. And how will they identify and represent them respectfully and accurately in a virtual setting?

5. Artistic manager

Maybe a musician, artist, textile arts expert, or someone familiar with island cultures. Keep in mind that several different individuals may fill these roles as this project is developed and executed. But there is undoubtedly going to be potential for people with overlapping skills to be effective and contribute (read: employed!)

You might be an architect interested in climate change who wants to get involved in preserving historical native structures so they can be enjoyed by future generations, even if only in a virtual environment.

Or perhaps your background is in marine biology, but you have a passion for managing complex projects that are tied to sustainability and environmental causes. And want to leverage virtual environments

Or you have developer or coding skills and experience building gaming environments but are looking to work in a setting that will have a broader socio-cultural impact than just teenage boys playing video games in their pajamas sitting on the couch at home.

Or maybe you have been working in a tightly controlled government or public sector setting and are itching to do something more impactful or to scratch that itch for working in an environment that is focused on preserving an ancient unique culture.

Or you are a creative person interested in ethnic and cultural artifacts. Joining this team on Tuvalu could be life-changing—putting you in a role where you are helping to keep a unique culture's music and art alive and preserve some historic artistic traditions that otherwise might be lost.

EXAMPLE #2: Amazon Looks to Sparrow to Carry Its Robotics Ambitions

Subheading: The e-commerce giant plans to use the new robot and others to automate more of its warehouses during a period of cost-cutting.[75]

Here is another example from an article in *The Wall Street Journal*. "The robotic device, known as Sparrow, is outfitted with suction cups and artificial intelligence software rather than the eyes and hands of human workers. It is the latest attempt by Amazon to automate more of its warehousing operations by turning some of the most physically challenging and repetitive tasks over to robots."

The obvious roles that jump out are tied to logistics, robots, AI-based software, and digital commerce. If you are interested in one or more of these topic areas, you might try to track down someone at Amazon on LinkedIn or even Indeed or Monster to see if they are hiring in one or more of these areas. Here are a few of the obvious and not obvious possible career opportunities to explore based on this news article.

1. **Robotics software designer**
   Amazon will need someone who can write code that allows these comparatively small and quite use case-specific robots to do the work of humans. The

implication is also that they will need "robot wranglers" to manage, manipulate, and update these devices—interact with whoever the vendor is, collect and levy business requirements to facilitate the development of Sparrow 2.0 and perform other managerial and client liaison tasks.

2. Logistics manager

This represents a logical extension of the existing process around how products arrive in warehouses, get selected, and ultimately shipped out to customers, but using this new technology to improve efficiency, reduce costs, and enhance productivity.

3. Organizational change consultant

Someone has to modify and update existing processes to work in settings where humans once reigned. In other words, determine how to connect humans, robots, and products in the most efficient and cost-effective way.

EXAMPLE #3: Metal Recycler Continuum Raises $36M in Funding [76]

This article in *Recycling Today* describes a company based in Silicon Valley that provides powered metal for 3D printing made from recycled materials. They are creating a circular metals economy critical to helping meet the world's sustainability goals. Think about the range of possible careers here based on this news article.

The company Continuum will certainly be looking for people interested in evolving 3D printing/additive manufacturing strategies and who are passionate about sustainability. Roles will include software developers and business development roles. If you are interested in the future of 3D printing and have a passion for recycling and reusing limited resources, you should go to their website and see if there are any openings!

EXAMPLE #4: Moon to Mars Initiative Round Three Grants Announced[77]

An article on the *Space Australia* website describes, "A further $3 million in grants have been announced by the Australian Space Agency in the third round of the Moon to Mars initiative grants, going to four Australian businesses, boosting Australia's space manufacturing and economy."

I remember a line in the movie *The Martian,* where Matt Damon is trying to figure out how he is going to survive after being abandoned and says he is going to have to "science the heck" out it—the problem that is.

Talk about a new set of career opportunities! This combines the space economy with rocket development with supporting non-terrestrial habitation. The potential roles are almost mind boggling.

Elon Musk and their team have demonstrated the viability of reusable rockets, which will almost certainly be required to make this work. Architectural firms will be engaged to design buildings that will probably be assembled by robots on the lunar surface. How will the Moon inhabitants feed themselves? Ag tech implications. Communications at a level not undertaken before. Lunar Logistics might be a startup looking to take advantage of this interest. Will there be a Moon Payload division at Maersk, the leader in supply chain and shipping logistics here on Terra Ferma?

EXAMPLE #5: Polarisqb and Auransa Announce Promising Results for Triple-negative Breast Cancer Using Quantum Computing and AI[78]

An article on the FirstWord HEALTHTECH website describes how these two companies' partnership represents a compelling example of historically disconnected disciplines connecting to deliver astonishing results and future careers.

One of these technologies—quantum computing—barely existed five years ago. Using quantum computers to identify candidate molecules that can cure various diseases ten times faster than was previously possible is a fantastic advancement of biomedicine.

If you are passionate about addressing women's health issues or previously intractable medical challenges, this might be a role for you. If you are excited about the range of applications for quantum-based solutions, you might visit their Career Page and see if there are any openings.

I lay these examples out as a real-world approach to identifying possible new careers to include in your ongoing lifelong investigation. Look for ways to apply this technique to your findings in the Future Career Toolkit exercises, especially the ANTENNA tool. Be on the lookout for these kinds of examples of cross-discipline roles that are emerging—and believe me, they are!

This leads us to the focus of the next chapter, our third Future Career Tool, MESH. This is where you track down the people who are working, thinking, writing, and speaking in the new career landscape. It's time to get in touch with them to start a dialogue! Get on their radar! MESH is how you combine the two tools VOICE and ANTENNA to deliver actual results: identify and get that next opportunity and enjoy a new career!

– CHAPTER 11 –

"MESH" With the Right People

> "Chance Favors the Prepared Mind."
> **French biologist and chemist Louis Pasteur[79]**

There is an old saying in showbiz that is becoming increasingly critical in the business community: "It's not what you know; it's who you know." While this is not a big revelation, in today's global borderless workplace, it is mission-critical to build a mega-network of friends and colleagues who can help you find your next career.

The exercise I'm going to share with you will help you focus on who you know and, more importantly, help you figure out who you do not know. The objective here is to start to identify people who can help you successfully navigate the next step of your career journey.

Chase the Innovators

No matter what field, there are *always* people at the forefront of any discipline. There is always a Miles Davis leading the charge and doing innovative things in any given area. You may have heard of this jazz legend but if not, put down this book right now and search for his music on YouTube. Seriously. His work is incredible. The Rock and Roll Hall of Fame called him a "trumpeter, visionary, and eternal modernist . . . a force of nature"[80] and *Rolling Stone* magazine once said he was "one of the most influential artists of the 20th century."[81] Other examples of people at the forefront of their discipline might include LeBron James (basketball), Greta Thunberg (climate awareness), and Billie Eilish (pop music).

So, believe me when I say you need to track down the Miles Davis of whatever field *you* are passionate about! There will be one: trust me. As I have mentioned before, today, there are thousands of publications and channels where leading thinkers talk, write, and speak about what is coming next in any given field. Ferreting them out was the work you did for the ANTENNA exercise. Now, it is time to connect with them.

Network, Network, Network

Networking is not a new thing. The success of humankind is based to a large degree on our ability to collaborate, leverage, and align our various skills. This is how movies are made, battleships are built, A.I. algorithms are developed, and armies conquer enemies. Put very simply, it is our ability to collaborate that has enabled humans to create advanced societies that drive the growth of culture, civilization, and technological innovations, from the wheel to the Space Shuttle.

Ancient humans may not have had the luxury of updating their social media status to let their family and friends know what they were up to. Still, different kinds of social networks were an essential component of their lives, nevertheless. In fact, James Fowler, the co-author of a 2018 study from Harvard University, *said,* "We found that what modern people are doing with online social networks is what we've always done, not just before Facebook, but before agriculture."[82]

Fowler and his colleague Nicholas Christakis (in their book *Connected: The Surprising Power of Our Social Networks and How They Shape Our Lives)* also show that our experience of the world depends on where we find ourselves within social networks. Studies have found that networks influence a surprising variety of lifestyle and health factors, such as how prone you are to obesity, how likely you are to quit smoking, how likely you are to experience happiness, and, of course, by implication, where you work!

The Ongoing Evolution of Twenty-First-Century Networking

How people will work in the future and how companies will operate are key considerations when designing a strategy for connecting with your mega-network. You need to understand the various options and tools and how to use them. While LinkedIn and other customer relationship management tools are the standard today, they will most certainly evolve, just like virtual reality, artificial intelligence, and telepresence robotics continue to complement our current communication, collaboration, and interaction toolsets.

Keep in mind, too, that thought leaders and influencers will inevitably change and evolve as well. People who were once considered at the top of their game in their chosen field are often usurped, often by someone younger (as much as I hate to say it) or even a person from an entirely different field.

In fact, an expression from my aforementioned music biz days in New York demonstrates the rise and fall of popularity and influence in a particular field.

A musician's career in New York often goes like this:
1. Who's Chris Bishop?
2. Get me Chris Bishop!
3. Get me a young Chris Bishop.
4. Who's Chris Bishop?

The same model often applies to *any* field. One minute, you're an unknown; the next, everyone wants to work with you; then, suddenly, everyone is looking for a younger version of you until, finally, no one remembers who you are. Yes, it sounds bleak, but it's often true, unfortunately.

Believe it or not, it even happened to the genius physicist and polymath Albert Einstein. By the end of his career, he had split from the mainstream physics community due in large part to his public rejection of the new theory of quantum mechanics. Because of this, few scientists in the field kept up with Einstein's later work. Toward the end of his life, "most physicists were starting to think of Einstein as a relic," according to Paul Halpern, University of the Sciences in Philadelphia.[83]

Applying this idea to the topic at hand, a thought leader emerges with a unique and valuable perspective and reveals a concept no one has thought of before. The person rides that wave for a while, and then someone comes along with the next iteration that upends or expands things. And so it goes: every discipline has this pattern.

This is all the more reason to have a robust and constantly evolving mega-network. It will be critical to your success as a worker in the new business models that are coming.

Using the (Current) Tools

Nowadays, more and more people are working in overlapping fields and across geographic borders and time zones. These people need to know people and have people know them all over the planet. Speaking from experience, over the course of my time at IBM in the early 2000s, I would often find myself on conference calls with people in Australia, Singapore, England, India, Germany, China, Belarus, New York, and California—all at the same time!

Expanding work opportunities will continue to exist all over the planet twenty-four hours a day, seven days a week, and 365 days a year. We have already seen a dramatic shift, driven by the global pandemic, toward using new tools like Zoom, Microsoft Teams, Skype, WebEx, and Google Meet to collaborate, interact, and conduct business in real-time all over the planet. That trend is only accelerating. It's the New Normal for workplace interaction.

Teams will continue to create solutions, address business problems, and share expertise from anywhere on the planet, from locations above the planet (think: the International Space Station), and most likely, at some point from the Moon, Mars, and maybe even from mining colonies on asteroids!

At present, apps and websites like Facebook, LinkedIn, X/Twitter, Instagram, WeChat, WhatsApp, and TikTok offer incredible ways to find people, share information, and collaborate on projects.

The bottom line is that tracking down potential employers, colleagues, and business partners who share your passion or level of curiosity around specific subjects is easier than ever. This is a model for communication that never existed before. And this new capability enables workers to shift roles and navigate a nonlinear career path reasonably easily.

Working as a freelance musician in New York City was where I learned the importance of building and maintaining a network the hard way. In that world, as in many roles where you are an individual with a certain talent, set of skills, and experience, you are only able to work based on *who you know.*

This happens in every industry. A photographer works with a stylist he likes. A producer hires a director she has worked with before. An ad agency assigns copywriters and art directors based on how likely they are to win the business not only with their skills but also their relationships. A financial services firm assigns managers to accounts where they have deep knowledge of a long-standing client or vertical, with the idea that the decision will ultimately translate into revenue.

Those connections are also how you make your next big career move.

Give to Get

At the end of the day, networking is a "quid pro quo" activity. Someone you know will also reach out to you based on your ability to drive their success forward. In turn, if you have the skills someone deems valuable to help them achieve whatever goals or objectives they may have, your odds of getting tapped improve immeasurably. In other words, make sure you have skills that can help someone (read: a client or employer) be successful.

Contrary to what you may have heard, clients and employers do not hire or recommend people just because they are friends. They recommend them in order to look savvy and smart and in touch with what their client or manager might need. Ultimately, you get selected or hired based on your skill set matching the hiring manager's or HR person's needs.

The MESH Exercise

One key objective of the MESH exercise is tracking down people who are providing future-focused thought leadership and insight: the ones who have a forward-thinking, innovative perspective about the field you are interested in and how it is trending.

The best candidates include people who:

- Have strategic roles at organizations where you might want to work.
- Have started companies you might want to join.
- Are leading organizations that you admire and respect, which could be private sector companies, foundations, government agencies, or non-profits.

These are the ones you want to connect with! The marketplace has rewarded them and, as a result, they are successful; they have identified and nurtured the right contacts. These are the people who can help *you* become successful. You can also use *their* connections to expand your network and brand recognition, so don't forget to look at the networks your contacts are in. I call this "Using the X/Twitter Math."

Check out who they follow on X/Twitter or Instagram. What LinkedIn Groups are they members of? Who do they think are important influencers? Search out their blogs or photostreams. What kinds of articles do they read and share? Glean, from their comments and posts, who they think Miles Davis is in their given field. Find out what they are focused on, their backgrounds, and who they think is advancing the thinking in your field of choice. This information represents a treasure trove of potential contacts that can help to build your own network.

And, just as I suggested with the other exercises, make this a daily habit. In fact, I would allocate twenty to thirty minutes a day for this kind of network-enhancing "sleuthing."

Even though there are many tools that are available, I recommend using LinkedIn for this particular activity. As of this writing, it is considered the "de facto" standard networking tool. It is where most professionals have at least some kind of profile. Not familiar with it? Try it out. Like other sites and apps, you can post pictures, videos, and text. People can comment on your posts and react to the content you share. LinkedIn is structured to make it simple to find people and contact them. In fact, I think that LinkedIn is the best place for expertise sharing, relationship building, connecting, and sharing your personal VOICE to build out your MESH.

Building Out Your MESH

Here are the steps to what I like to refer to as "building out your MESH," using the topics, sources, and criteria identified in the VOICE and ANTENNA exercises.

PEOPLE

VOICE ATTRIBUTE	SOURCE	DESCRIPTION	FREQUENCY

GROUP

STEP 1: Start by identifying the right people who can help you.

Use sources identified in your ANTENNA exercise to initially select interesting *people* to connect with.

Again, my recommendation is to start with LinkedIn. For academics, professors and researchers, try searching university websites. Some well-known bloggers and authors provide ways to reach them in their "About Me" section. Don't be afraid to get resourceful! Find a way to track down someone you want to connect with. Use X/Twitter, YouTube, Vimeo, Instagram, Pinterest, Bluesky, blogs, Wikipedia, websites, etc.

Here is a checklist you might follow:

1. First, do a LinkedIn search for people working in the areas you are interested in. Your criteria might include their professional title, area of focus, location, etc. Use quotes to include multiple criteria in one search.
    - Try to find three to five people you know in the fields you are interested in.
    - Second, pick two to three people who are one degree of separation away.
    - Third, pick one to two who are two degrees of separation away.
2. Next, send them each a "Connection Request."
    - Scrutinize their profile to tease out information to use in a note introducing yourself.
    - Always personalize the message—keep the tone professional but engaging; sound excited about who they are and what they do.
    - If possible, mention someone you know that they also know, or cite other things you may connect on: where they went to college, where

they worked before their current company, a topic of shared interest, et al.
- Describe something interesting you did recently, a topic you wrote about, or an event you attended/spoke at that connects to their area of expertise or interest.

3. Once you connect with them, ask if they'd be willing to meet with you for a thirty-minute "Informational Interview." If they are local, it could be in person for coffee or lunch, or via a video conferencing tool like Zoom, WebEx, Teams, or Google Meet if they are far away.

4. Do additional research on the person to prepare for your "Informational Interview" and jot down some questions to ask about what they do, what their other areas of interest are, and what they are working on; also, prepare to succinctly describe your own background in order to discuss topics of shared interest.

5. When you get the chance, mention that you are always exploring new opportunities and ask them to please keep you in mind if a role opens up on their team, in their organization, or with a colleague's organization.

6. Add their contact information to your Customer Relationship Management tool (a place where you store your contacts and track your interactions . . . more on this later)

7. Based on the meeting's outcome, make a note to contact them again in a week, ten days, or a month (you pick a time frame) as a follow-up.
8. My advice? Use this checklist to try to add five people a week to your LinkedIn profile.

STEP 2: Search for three to five groups to join.

Search on LinkedIn under Groups and Companies by topic area, location, vertical, discipline, company name, technology, etc.

1. Observe the topics being discussed to see how closely they align with your own areas of interest.
2. Take note of how large the groups are: a small number of members means fewer opportunities to grow your network; try to only join large groups with lots of activity.
3. See who is in the group: hopefully, several well-regarded thought leaders, writers, speakers, or successful business people are members of the groups you select.
4. If the group meets your criteria, ask to join. Some require you to "request" membership; most will readily let you in.
5. Check in on these communities at least once every week to ten days to see what kinds of conversations are happening.
6. It is OK to simply lurk on the sidelines, but don't hesitate to look for opportunities where you can weigh in, share your perspective, make a comment

on someone's contribution, or start your own conversation thread.

7. Look closely at who the members are once you have joined and reach out to any who are making interesting and insightful contributions to the conversations. Observe who might be in senior roles in their organization (read: they can hire you!) Ask them to connect.

Here is an example of what my **MESH** chart would look like, based on the data collected through the **VOICE** and **ANTENNA** exercises.

PEOPLE

VOICE ATTRIBUTE	SOURCE	DESCRIPTION	FREQUENCY
Future culture	Gerd Leonhardt	CEO	Futures Agency
Tech	Krysta Svore	GM, Quantum Software	Microsoft
Global business	Thomas Malone	Professor, author	MIT Sloan

GROUP

Future culture	Institute for the Future	https://www.linkedin.com/groups/2359154/

Search for Events to Attend

Even though we are living in an increasingly "virtually" connected world, there is still something to be said for getting together with other carbon-based life forms in the same physical space! These kinds of interactions allow you to meet people you might never have connected with otherwise. You just might experience serendipitous encounters with people whose areas of focus are the same as your own. Or you might run into people with similar interests who also believe in the power of in-person networking. Plus, real-life interactions can be fun!

There are many ways to do this, from local Meetups to large-scale global events. To get a sense of options, do a simple Google search on events related to your areas of interest. Add qualifying criteria to narrow your results. These might include a specific vertical (retail, tech, aerospace), a specific computer language or toolset (Java, Python, Lisp, Prolog, or C++), a specific discipline (marketing, legal, operations, media), or a specific geography (local, big US cities, international).

You can also do a search on Meetups' website. Simply put in the topic, your zip code, and the VOICE qualifiers you came up with, and see what pops up. There is even guidance on how to host your own Meetup if you do not find one locally that appeals to you.

Eventbrite.com allows you to use specific criteria to search for events you might want to attend. You can sort them by category ("science and tech" might be a good place to start), event type (conference, convention, expo) and price (free or paid). You will find many events to choose from. And once you have entered your search criteria, you can opt-in to be notified when similar events are taking place in the future.

One note to keep in mind: many of the more significant events, especially ones where high-profile, famous people speak, can be awfully expensive. But! Most of them also welcome volunteers. A technique that I have used with great success in the past is to reach out to the event organizers and simply offer to help. Many of these organizations are stretched thin and will welcome the opportunity to engage someone who is interested in the conference topic!

As a volunteer, you might be asked to help with registration, wrangle microphones for speakers and panels, help move and arrange signage, set up/break down various displays, and even get a keynote speaker a bottle of the sparkling water they prefer if that is what is required. But it would all be worth it: you would be able to attend the event for free and have a chance to hear from experts speaking about a topic you are interested in, not to mention the opportunity to expand your network by introducing yourself in person to someone you admire. Simply put, try to attend, participate (for the cost of travel and an Airbnb), and expand your MESH network.

Keeping Track of Everybody: The Power of a Customer Relationship Management System

As you expand your network, you will need a way to keep track of who you talked with, sent an email to, or had coffee with . . . as well as who *did not respond* to your email or phone call. While everyone has their own method of keeping track of info, I strongly encourage you to investigate a digital solution that is portable and operating system agnostic.

I use a cloud-based Customer Relationship Management tool called "Less Annoying CRM," or "LA CRM." It is perfect for me. But there are many options for you to try out: Copper, Act!, Zoho, and many others. These tools are technically designed to support salespeople, but they are easily adapted to general networking. And being a cloud-based tool, LA CRM and others like it, are accessible from anywhere through a browser. Most of these tools have a mobile version designed for your smartphone.

I use this tool *every day* to keep track of the people I work with. You can set up Pipelines to monitor and organize people by their roles or objectives, whatever classification works best for you. I also have people organized in different in-app Calendars based on criteria like writing projects, speaking engagements, workshop sponsors, tech gurus, movers and shakers, and innovative educators, just to name a few.

But really, you can use any tool you prefer, whatever helps you keep track of who you are talking to, what you discussed in that conversation, the next steps and follow-up activities, a contact's value, and who they might know that you could then contact regarding your work.

As you are on your way to building out your MESH network and looking for your next career, keep in mind that a job hunt is a numbers game. The model is like a snail mail direct mailing campaign: if you send out a hundred flyers and one person responds, you are doing well. If three people respond, you are incredibly lucky. Don't get discouraged! Keep at it. Some contacts will be dead ends. It could be people who either do not respond for whatever reason or with whom there is not a strong enough alignment between your skills and what they want to achieve. There may be any number of other reasons someone doesn't get back to you. But do not be put off. Keep pushing. Find three people to replace the person who is not responding.

A Lifelong Job

You don't ever wake up one morning and say, "OK, that's it. I am finally *done* networking. I can relax now. My MESH is complete. I know everyone I need to know."

Trust me. This will NEVER happen.

To succeed, you need to create a routine to monitor and manage your MESH development and plan to do it *long-term*. Set a checkpoint for 5 p.m. every Friday. If you have not added at least five people by then, get to it. Put down the Gameboy, log out of Twitch, stop binging on Netflix, postpone the snipe on eBay.

The more people who know who you are, what you are interested in, and what your talents and experience are, the better your odds will be for successfully navigating your next career.

Your network only grows and grows as you move from career to career, make new friends, have a family, or travel the globe. Creating a robust MESH of connected contacts lays the groundwork for future employment and a lifelong path through multiple careers. You see, people in hiring roles or entrepreneurs who are building companies are always looking for talented people. The more people who know who you are, the higher your odds of getting hired. And because the products and services at companies are constantly morphing to meet market needs and chase revenue opportunities, their internal job economy is also constantly in flux. Having a mega network—your MESH—increases the odds of being thought of and eventually hired. You may not get the job you applied for, but at some point, the hiring manager or start-up CEO might create a role where your skills and experience would be perfect. But they must know who you are to hire you!

The more people who know who you are and what you are interested in, the more people understand your unique passion, talent, and commitment, the better your odds of landing somewhere doing something interesting again and again and again.

– CHAPTER 12 –

Taking the Long View

> "I welcome our computer overlords"
> —Ken Jennings, Jeopardy Grand Champion after being crushed by IBM Watson in 2011[84]

> "The times they are a-changin'"
> —Bob Dylan

You, dear reader, are a player in a continuum. Most of the people in my parents' generation were groomed to work in one role at one company for an entire career. I spent fifteen years at IBM and worked with people who had been there twenty-five, thirty, thirty-five, even forty years! Many were smart and talented. But too many of them got really good at doing one thing: working at IBM! They learned how to game the annual performance review. They figured out which execs to suck up to and which ones to avoid. They scammed ways to take personal credit for a successful team effort or learned how to make someone else appear responsible when their project failed or if an exec was unhappy.

Those days are gone.

Admittedly, right now, we only have the view from where we sit in the early twenty-first century. In 2035, however, the view could be completely different. And it will have shifted again in 2055. Shifted to what? We can only imagine. But you can count on the fact that there will be a whole new set of companies, players, business models, career options, and skill needs that we can't even fathom yet. These will determine the way we work. As a result, the work model will be transformed yet again. The times are a-changin' indeed! And will continue to.

I want to give a concrete example of how this works today. An open job req on the Career page for Rigetti, a leading quantum computer company, is a real-world example of exactly what I am talking about.

It is titled Future Open Position and says, "Don't see an open position that fits your background? Apply here so we can keep your resume on file for future opportunities!" This approach has tremendous implications for jobs that don't exist yet! Leading companies are already realizing that they don't know what kinds of skills and talent will be needed as their business models evolve. But they want to be ready by building a roster of smart, interested potential employees!

Embrace What's Coming

As we've seen, technology drives human progress, business models, skill needs, and careers, and it has been that way for thousands of years. But throughout history, technological advancements have also consistently helped us gain unique insights, improve how we live, and transform how we work and what we do for a living. So, my advice? Embrace the tech you have access to today. But also keep in mind that it will change and morph and evolve. Be prepared to decipher and embrace the next evolution. Keep an eye out for what's coming next.

The Key Takeaways

As we wrap things up, I want to remind you of a few key points from this book that I hope you will carry with you throughout your long and successful set of careers.

1. Stay on top of emerging trends, both from a technology perspective and across a range of different industries and verticals.
2. Get out of your comfort zone! Once you are acclimated to your current job, start looking for your next one!
3. Search out learning resources in unexpected places. Remember that those resources will constantly be morphing.
4. Identify career opportunities where disciplines are intersecting in new and surprising ways! Think about medicine and mechanical engineering. Mull over the idea of hospitality meeting astrophysics. Ponder robotics and the law.
5. Leverage what you know. Be honest about what you don't know and then figure out how to bridge the gap.

6. Be proactive and creative when inventing the next career you can be passionate about. And the one after that. And the one after that.

So, In Conclusion...

When I conduct my workshops, I always end things in a very deliberate way. I turn to the assembled throng, give it a two-beat pause, and then say excitedly, "*You* are going to do stuff that is going to look like magic to me! So, get to it! I want to see some of your amazing handiwork!"

My meta objective with this book, dear reader, is to get *you* excited about the amazing handiwork *you're* going to be creating in the new workplace paradigm that's coming. I hope my musings have provided some socio-historical perspective and that my personal career journey has helped you expand your awareness of what is possible.

We are at a tipping point, and you are empowered to advance society and culture more than any previous generation. You are equipped to drive innovation in the twenty-first century's global borderless workplace and beyond.

In Summary...

It has been an interesting journey so far, to say the least. Keep in mind that as you navigate *your* own career paths, you will always need to be aware of the gap between what you know and what you will need to learn how to do in the future. The lifelong requirement is to then discover where and how to acquire those skills.

I hope this book has helped you imagine the wide range of possible future career paths that await you and that I have made the steps to get there a little less daunting. I look forward to hearing about your exciting and successful future careers.

So, get to it! Find that amazing next career and make some magic!

AFTERWORD

My Story

Back in the 1950s, a famous broadcaster named Paul Harvey used to conclude his feature reports on little-known topics with the catchphrase, "And now you know the *rest* of the story." I have definitely sprinkled some personal anecdotes throughout this book, but now it's time you know the rest of my story. If nothing else, it will give you some context for the career search exercises I shared with you. And, if you're struggling to regain your footing after a job loss or simply trying to imagine starting on a whole new career path, I think you may find some similarities and hopefully some encouragement.

This chapter contains my own personal stories about my journey through several careers. I've also included what I call "Teachable Moments," lessons that I learned at moments of transition in my life that perhaps you can apply to your own career search today and in the future.

I won't be insulted if you skip this chapter, or if you read other parts of the book first and come back here from time to time looking for a little storytelling. Some editors and publishing professionals have tried to talk me out of including this chapter. One senior publishing exec derisively described the content as "throat-clearing."

After mulling it over, I decided to leave the stories in. Ray Dalio, in his book, "Principles."[85] issued a similar disclaimer about including his own background. I found his personal story fascinating, *and* it helped me to better contextualize the concepts he talks about in his book. At the end of the day, a voice inside said, "Just be candid, man, and tell the story."

So, here's looking at you, Ray. Here's my story.

The Journey Begins

I would argue that *my* career journey has been pretty interesting so far, if I must say so myself. Also, I hope that hearing me describe my various twists, turns, triumphs, and heartaches alike makes what advice I have to share with you that much more real, dear reader. (Don't worry! I saved the most salacious stories for after the obituary).

I was born in the summer of 1950, along with my twin sister Suzanne, in the early throes of the now infamous Baby Boomer explosion. I spent my childhood and teenage years growing up with my twin and our younger sister Kim in a lovely (but quite remote) town in upstate New York. Glens Falls is situated in the foothills of the Adirondacks just south of beautiful Lake George and north of Saratoga, where the famous racetrack is.

Like most of America in the early 1960s, Glens Falls was roaring along in the post-WWII boom. Our town had a paper pulp mill, a lace manufacturing plant, and a contingent of professionals—doctors, lawyers, executives, and teachers. There was also a robust local theater group called The Operetta Club, which is, in fact, where my parents met. We always had records of the soundtracks to current Broadway shows playing in the living room!

Left Brain/Right Brain

I was always a left brain/right brain kind of kid, really into science but also into music and performing. I loved playing classical and band music. But I also have fond memories of creating a report on gamma rays for the science club when I was in seventh grade and thinking it was the coolest topic ever. I mean, they are at the extreme end of the electromagnetic spectrum *and behave in totally unique ways!*

I had been taking advanced math classes, and I wore the obligatory crewcut and black-framed glasses with various pieces of tape holding them together at all times. Yep, I was that kid.

As I said, my parents had met in our local community theater. My dad was a great singer with an extraordinary flair for show tunes, as well as hymns in church as a soloist. He had a big rolling tenor voice and used to sing along out loud at the movies or in any public setting whenever he was so moved, much to my younger self's horror. My mom played piano and acted and sang. There was always music and theater in our house. In fact, Suzanne and I got into a little bit of trouble for consistently interrupting our second-grade class activities by performing show tunes our parents had been working on. At one point, our teacher called our mother and asked if she could please "discourage the twins from their in-class musical performances." Ha!

Ladies and Gentlemen... *The Beatles!*

After experiencing an intense dislike for piano lessons at age five, I started playing the trumpet in third grade and then the baritone horn in junior high school, mostly because no one was playing that instrument. I also dabbled in French horn one summer. But my true musical revelation came on a Sunday evening in February 1964.

I'll never forget it: I was in my grandmother's sitting room (yes, Calista Caldow—who I mentioned in the Introduction!) watching her old black-and-white television. It was cold and blustery outside, and our family had decided to stay after dinner to watch *The Ed Sullivan Show,* a mainstay of American family entertainment in the early 1960s. I had heard something about a new band from England, but my thirteen-year-old self didn't know what was about to happen.

Then, suddenly, the Beatles appeared on the screen with their wacky haircuts and cool collarless suits. Girls in the audience were screaming at the top of their lungs, but what I really noticed were the songs: wonderful, catchy, upbeat, and fun! The overall vibe—that feeling of four guys working on something together, making a sound that each of them contributed to—absolutely transfixed me.

And then it transformed me. That moment began what I now call my twenty-year digression into the music business.

The next day, I dug out my dad's old acoustic guitar from under his bed and began to teach myself to play using a Beatles Songbook I bought at the local music store. Soon, I put my first band together. We did covers of Beatles' songs and stuff from The Rolling Stones. We performed songs by The Doors, Jimi Hendrix, The Beach Boys and more. We dabbled in the artistry of the great blues masters like Chuck Berry, Muddy Waters, and Howlin' Wolf. As I got older, I put a more edgy rock band together, and we did gigs at my high school, at CYO dances, and at Battle of the Bands events all over upstate New York and Vermont.

I admired and emulated John Lennon, but one day at rehearsal, the bass player announced that he was as good as he was going to get. Frustrated, I decided to buy a bass guitar and learn how to play it, thinking that whatever band I was in would always have a bass player. I ended up doing it for a living for over twenty years. And I still play!

When I was a senior in high school, I was invited to join a legendary local rock band made up of older, more seasoned musicians. It involved playing five nights a week at a local club where it was illegal for me to work because I was only seventeen. Shockingly, after some hesitation, my parents actually agreed to let me do this.

So, for the last semester of high school, I'd come home in the afternoon, do some homework, maybe take a nap, and then go to the gig from 8 p.m. until midnight during the week. On Friday and Saturday, the hours were more like 9 p.m. to 1 a.m. After four grueling months of this, I ended up in the hospital for ten days with jaundiced mononucleosis.

Still, it was a really fun experience, and it was excellent training for me as a musician, interacting with fans and working with seasoned players.

Designing a Learning Path

I would have to say a seminal moment that influenced the rest of my life was being accepted to Bennington College.

Bennington is a small liberal arts school with five hundred students in southwestern Vermont. Over its storied history, many legendary artists and innovative thinkers taught there: Peter Drucker, Jackson Pollack, and Kenneth Noland. Legendary comic and actress Carol Channing is an alum. *Game of Thrones* Peter Dinklage went there. Martha Graham taught dance in the 1930s.

The real differentiating factor for me was the fact that students were required to basically design their own education. Starting with your Junior year, you were expected to formulate a plan for what you were going to study, articulate who was going to teach you, and describe what the final outcome was going to be. It had to be charted over your final two years at the college. And you not only had to create, design, and formulate this plan, but you then had to defend it in front of a tribunal of teachers and administrators. I discovered that this was a perfect setting for me. I had a pretty clear idea of what I wanted to learn and how I was going to learn it, as well as who was going to help me, from a faculty perspective as well as fellow students.

This is where I learned how to identify what skills I wanted or needed to acquire and formulate a strategy for acquiring them. This was where I began to understand my own strengths and weaknesses.

TEACHABLE MOMENT #1

At the risk of sounding like a commercial, the lessons I learned as a student at Bennington College laid the groundwork for processes that I have successfully used to navigate my career path to date. In fact, they form the basis of my Future Career Toolkit (see Chapters 9–11), which I have refined and updated based on the numerous real-world situations I have found myself in. These are lessons that I hope you, dear reader, can exploit for your own career journey!

Key Takeaway: *Learn how to learn. Learn who to talk to. Learn what tools and resources are available—or not available. Use them. And then be prepared to do it all again.*

Looking For a Mind at Work, Work, Work...

After a few months at Bennington, I decided I wanted to really focus on music. But it's worth noting that I actually majored in German literature—that is what my degree is in!

I wanted to expand my knowledge of not only the bass but also acquire skills in composition and arranging and expand my horizons when it came to music in general. I rented an upright string bass, found a teacher, and began learning how to play classical music on the instrument. After practicing sometimes as much as four hours a day, within a year, I got the role of Associate Principal Contrabass with the Berkshire Symphony at Williams College just down the road.

But I was also hungry to learn more about jazz, the history of the genre, and its artists. So, I studied with Bill Dixon, a professor at Bennington who was a well-regarded free jazz trumpet player and composer from New York. One of my most incredible musical experiences occurred when Bill arranged to have jazz great John Coltrane's bass player, Jimmy Garrison, come to the school for a semester. (P.S. If you are unfamiliar with Coltrane, head to your nearest music app and investigate; you won't be sorry!)

I got to play my upright bass in Jimmy's ensemble and even took private lessons from him! His groove and sound and feel were as you might imagine—magical! It was an incredible learning experience for a young rock 'n roll guy from upstate New York.

When I was not performing jazz or classical, I was playing pop music. I put together a rock band to play in Vermont ski lodges, and we covered the hits of the day from The Rolling Stones, Creedence Clearwater Revival, Elton John, and old rock 'n roll and blues tunes.

TEACHABLE MOMENT #2

This was one of my first 'multimodal' experiences—playing music across three different and distinct genres at the same time. And not only feeling comfortable about it but also enjoying the range of expressive options. You, dear reader, have the same innate capacity, and I encourage you to explore it! In today's era of the gig economy and the side hustle, this is a meta-model for today's workers.

An Early Lesson in the Power of Connections

My next major transition (and proverbial "lucky break") took place after graduating from college. At this point, I learned an early lesson about the importance of your network (what I call MESH in my Future Career Toolkit).

I was sleeping on the couch at my parents' house. I had no idea what I would do for a living and had been rejected after applying for several private school music teacher jobs outside of Boston. It was the holiday season, and many musician friends from my childhood were back in Glens Falls to visit their families. Paul—a great guitar player from that band of older kids I played with in high school—invited me to a jam with him and a local drummer who had gone to New York and gotten some good gigs. (This guy actually played on the first Hall and Oates record and went on to tour and record with Meatloaf and Todd Rundgren for many years).

Anyway, we jammed at his house, and it felt *great*.

The next day, Paul was talking to a friend of his who was the guitar player for a band called McKendree Spring. They had been touring and opening for acts like Elton John at The Fillmore East. By then, they had recorded four albums and were looking for a new bass player. Paul told his friend that he had just played with me and that I sounded pretty good after my years of training in college.

Now I had gone to hear McKendree Spring at various local gigs because they first put the band together at the local community college. And I really loved their first album. So, when I got a call to fly down to Ithaca for an audition, I was thrilled.

Secretly I convinced myself that Paul's friend was just being nice by giving me a chance and figured they would hire a New York or LA. "session guy" to go on the road with them. I resolved not to get my hopes up.

Much to my surprise, they called me a couple of days later and offered me the gig!

I ended up spending three years touring with them. We did some amazing shows as headliners and opened for acts like ZZ Top, The Eagles, Fleetwood Mac, Frank Zappa, Weather Report, and Linda Ronstadt, among many others. We also recorded three albums, including some of my own tunes. After doing my first record with them at The Manor outside of Oxford, England, we did the next one at Jimi Hendrix's Electric Ladyland studio in New York and then another album at Bearsville in Woodstock, where Bob Dylan and The Band had recorded. I was living my dream.

TEACHABLE MOMENT #3

*It is always important to cultivate relationships with people who are successful. This may sound crass at first, but it is a key tenant of my overall philosophy. Even if you don't particularly like someone, that's okay. If the world has recognized their talents and rewarded them with success, **those** are the people you need to align with. By knowing Paul, I was able to get the opportunity of a lifetime.*

Learning to Be a Pro

Being a musician at a professional level posed a new set of challenges and required several tweaks to my skillset. It also presented a serious learning curve. For starters, writing songs that were going to be on an actual record was a totally different discipline than composing cute ditties for myself and my current girlfriend. Playing and singing at a consistently high level in front of tens of thousands of people night after night was also new to me. Getting along with the other members of the band, living out of a suitcase for 185 days a year, traveling almost constantly, and dealing with an endless stream of Holiday Inns, rental cars, airport lounges, dressing rooms, and performance venues wore me out after a while.

I also learned the importance of being courteous and upbeat when interacting with fans at the gigs, many of whom had followed the band for years and had seen them perform with the two previous bass players. Rubbing shoulders with famous headliners like the Eagles, ZZ Top, Fleetwood Mac, and Frank Zappa was also a nerve-wracking tightrope walk; after all, how much interaction did they want to have with the opening act . . . and you with them? It varied widely, to be honest. The members of Fleetwood Mac, for example, were relaxed and friendly. The Eagles treated us like we were busboys.

Additionally, making records in a studio requires a high level of concentration, focus, and consistency. And then there were managers, producers, recording engineers, record company execs, and promoters. Learning how to act and interact in this new world took some adjusting and learning. But I was able to watch and listen and figure it out. Despite there being many challenging moments, I loved it. It was probably my favorite career of all of them . . . so far!

TEACHABLE MOMENT #4

When you are in a new setting, quickly identify the gaps in your skillset and figure out a plan to address them. What skills do you need to have, and where can you learn them? They may cover a new and much broader range than you were used to in your previous role, but it will be worth it. This has been a theme for me for all my careers. And it will be for you, too, dear reader. Embrace the gap, and don't be afraid to jump in. As often happens, McKendree Spring's life cycle followed a traditional bell curve regarding how bands form, evolve and break up. First, you're unknown, but one day, you find yourself getting a record deal and touring to play in front of larger and larger audiences. Then, promoters stop booking you because you're not selling enough records. This translates to playing in smaller and smaller venues and, eventually, you don't get the next record deal. Members start wanting to do other things, and then the band breaks up. That is precisely what happened to McKendree Spring after my third album with them.

I was twenty-five years old and had, for all intents and purposes, been fired. At that point, I was stuck in Ithaca, New York, not exactly a place with plentiful opportunities for aspiring musicians.

I had to figure out what to do next.

So, I signed up for a job delivering the local newspaper, The Ithaca Journal. In my beat-up Plymouth Valiant, I left my house every day at 4 p.m. and drove around putting copies of the paper in tubes next to mailboxes. This continued for months while I tried to figure out my next move. Was it my favorite gig? No. Did it keep me afloat until I could form a game plan? Yes. And I want to take a minute to assure you, dear reader, that there's nothing wrong with doing something similar if the situation calls for it. But I digress.

I soon made up my mind to move to New York City to see if I could "run with the big dogs" of the music scene. I knew many talented bass players were in the city, but I also had several friends who had moved there. I arrogantly (and probably a bit naively) thought that I, too, might be able to make a living working as a bass player in the city.

There's No Business Like Show Business

In those days, one of the hard, real-world lessons I learned was that "getting the job *is* the job." And the only way to get the job is to network.

I arrived in NYC in October 1976 and moved into a funky loft on Reade Street in lower Manhattan, in TriBeCa before it became TriBeCa. The apartment was above a store and had been rented by a sax player with whom I went to college. In those days, I actually slept *under the stairs* on a futon behind a curtain we had rigged up for privacy. (Take that, Harry Potter).

I found myself in the middle of a downtown musician community that was very welcoming and cool. Everyone was into jam sessions and trying to figure out what the music scene in New York was all about. Often, my friends and I would play music all night before wandering over to a bakery on West Broadway to get fresh, hot donuts. That was the jazz life!

But I also knew I needed to make some money, so one of the first things I did after settling in was to call an electric bass player named Will Lee. I met Will on the road three years earlier when he was playing with Horace Silver at a Dayton, Ohio club. McKendree Spring was opening for Billy Preston at the local arena.

I like to think of Will as the Einstein of the electric bass. Every time I see him perform, he does six things I have never seen him do before. Every. Time. And I have been watching and listening to him for years. Will has also played on literally hundreds of albums with famous artists like James Brown, Barbra Streisand, Cher, Ringo Starr, Chaka Khan, and Bette Midler—to name just a few. Not to mention that he performed as part of David Letterman's late-night talk show band for over thirty years!

So I gave him a call.

"Hello, this is Will!"

"Hey, man, I did it," I said. "I'm in New York. What do I do now?!"

Despite the fact that he was already quite famous and successful, Will was never full of himself or arrogant; just very helpful and unassuming. He replied without missing a beat.

"Schedule six jam sessions a day and panic to get to the next one. Eventually, one will turn into a gig."

He paused as I drew in a sharp breath. "Wow . . . okay . . ."

"Then do five jam sessions and the gig," he continued. "Then, you'll get two gigs. Next, do four jam sessions and the two gigs. See where I'm going with this?"

I did. What he was saying was, you have to do whatever it takes to build your "mega-network" in order for people to know who you are and what you can bring to an opportunity (More on that in Chapter 11: Building the MESH).

I took Will's advice, playing with dozens of different musicians in all kinds of settings and styles. Eventually, I took calls for everything, from jazz gigs playing string bass with a piano player at the Blarney Stone bar on West 72nd Street to traveling to Puerto Rico to perform with a country-western band at Officers Clubs on Army bases.

But I also got very lucky! Based on a referral from another college buddy, I landed a steady six-night-a-week gig playing with three Israelis at Club Ibis, an Egyptian cabaret on East 51st Street. There were two Vegas-style floor shows a night and the gig was from 9 p.m. to 3 a.m. It paid $300 a week!

Ready to Adapt

To make a living as a musician in New York City, I had to play just about every style there is. Now, some musicians I have encountered were only comfortable playing one or two styles. In fact, I once met this incredible bassist who was so dedicated to jazz that he drove a cab rather than compromise and play any other kind of music!

To me, this seems incredibly naive and foolish. But to each his own. Me? I have played classical, be-bop, funk/R&B, free jazz, country Western, pop-rock, techno, Irish,

Broadway, heavy metal, jazz standards, Middle Eastern, punk, bluegrass, and fusion. I had to develop strategies to acquire these skills along the way.

And I sometimes learned these lessons the hard way.

One memorable instance occurred when I was invited to join a jam session with a renowned Japanese jazz guitar player named Matsuo. When I arrived at his apartment in the West Village, he asked me what tunes I wanted to play. I said I didn't really know any be-bop tunes or standards. So, he pulled out some lead sheets, and I fumbled my way, sight-reading through a style I was completely unfamiliar with. Later on, I basically left that session with my tail between my legs.

Worse still, a few days later, I was in another jam session and overheard the guitar player talking to the sax player in the group.

"Hey, did you hear about the session at Matsuo's this week? The bass player didn't know any tunes! Do you believe that? What a lame-ass character he must be!"

I let a moment go by before jumping into the conversation.

"Yeah, that was me," I admitted. "I don't know any tunes . . . yet."

As a result of this embarrassing encounter, I reached out to a dear friend and amazing musician I knew from college who had also moved to New York. I told him what had happened and asked if he would teach me what I needed to know. I studied with him for several months. In addition, I also took classes to improve my sight-reading. This was a real-world situation where it became painfully clear that I had a skills gap that I needed to address if I was going to progress to the next level in my career.

TEACHABLE MOMENT #5

*Leverage your network: your friends, colleagues, peers, etc. Nine times out of ten, they will be willing to help you be successful, or they can send you to people who can point you in the right direction. Then, nurture your network, no matter what the situation. This is especially important if you are trying to transition to a new career. It is not **what** you know, but **who** you know and who knows **you**. That is how you will advance. It is a never-ending job, and it requires focus.*

So, there I was, a few years later, living the life of a successful freelance musician. I networked and played jam sessions, and I eventually ended up touring the world with some big names in music, including Robert Palmer, Ronnie Spector, and Darius Brubeck. But, one day, I arrived back in New York exhausted, tired of sleeping in hotels and waiting in various airport lounges to head to the next gig. So, I asked various friends in the music business about possible next steps for my career.

"Hey, what do I do to sleep in my own bed at night?"

They said, "Jingles, Man. Ya' gotta break into the session scene."

"The Jingle Biz" sounded like the dream life after years on the road. It meant playing on radio and TV commercials.

It meant working during normal business hours and playing fairly simple music, as long as you're a good sight-reader. It also meant doing recording sessions in a studio and getting paid a regular wage, along with residual checks when the commercials were renewed or revised. It sounded amazing after performing the last set at 2 a.m. in an Irish pub thousands of miles from home.

So, I decided to set my sights on breaking into "The Jingle Biz."

Of course, there were no tools like LinkedIn or Upwork back then. No X/Twitter or Instagram. There were only 3x5 paper index cards. I bought a box of them and kept track of all my interactions with musicians, copyists, recording engineers, copywriters, art directors, and music producers… everyone I could track down who was even remotely involved in the studio scene. And then, I called them all and asked each of them for three names. And then I called *those* people. I left messages and sent them all demo reels of my work. I visited their offices. And then I called them again. Later, I would send them an updated demo. I would visit their offices again. Sometimes, I took them to lunch.

Eventually, a music producer at an advertising agency called Backer Spielvogel hired me to play on a Miller Genuine Draft beer commercial.

Whew! I was in.

TEACHABLE MOMENT #6

Be ready to embrace changing life priorities to make a career change. Trust your instincts. Don't be afraid to admit that you want different things than you might have desired a few years ago, perhaps wanting to live in a different way and focus on a new set of life objectives.

Ch-Ch-Changes: The Year Music Became Data

I was cruising along, playing on jingles, and doing the occasional gig when suddenly everything changed. It was subtle at first. Then within eighteen months, literally the entire session scene in New York was upended completely.

In 1985, music became data.

Samplers, sequencers, and MIDI (Musical Instrument Digital Interface) all arrived on the scene and made it so that one musician could do the work of ten...or more. The ability to capture musical instruments onto a digital recording device or a hard drive completely changed the model for how music was created. The music scene went from a flourishing community of talented musicians doing recording sessions and live gigs to one person rolling in a rack full of digital equipment and playing everyone's part. The availability of personal computers and new software that could sample real instruments and create performances using sequencing software suddenly changed everything.

To be honest, it was depressing at first. And looking back, it must have been similar to how all of those farriers and blacksmiths felt way back in 1908 when Henry Ford started rolling Model Ts out of his Detroit factory: "That's a really great skill you guys have, but we just don't need people who know how to do that anymore."

But it was also an "Aha!" moment for me, a revelation that *all* business models morph and evolve. Before the change, there had been work for many people with specific skills. Then suddenly, the people with those specific skills, including bass players such as myself, were simply no longer needed. Instead, they were replaced by people with a *new* set of skills, people who knew how to create music on a computer and manipulate sound as information.

TEACHABLE MOMENT #7

Technology transforms every business model and has for literally thousands of years. Today, the forces at work include robotics, self-driving vehicles, drones, and—my personal favorite—quantum information science. This process of tech innovation driving business and cultural transformation will never change. You, dear reader, need to understand and embrace this fact, and you need to use it to your advantage.

Jingle All the Way ... to the World Wide Web

Based on this complete transformation of the music business, I bought a Mac Plus and learned how to compose on it. I learned how to stripe a tape with SMPTE time code so it could chase lock to picture and track video to audio for TV commercials. I began writing music using current technology. But it became clear that there was more consolidation going on and that if I *really* wanted to continue being some kind of a musician, I needed to go all in and embrace this new model for how music was being created.

In 1990, at the age of forty, I got my first "real job," where I needed to be someplace at a specific time every day. I was working at a jingle house in New York with a producer who owned a digital musical instrument called a "Synclavier," a state-of-the-art device at the time. He had been the musical director for the famous vocal group The Four Seasons for several years, and as a result, was able to purchase this really amazing (read: expensive!) instrument. Next, he set up a small studio near Union Square on lower Park Avenue South.

I had done a few free-lance sessions for him so when I proposed working at his jingle house, he was initially surprised. He thought of me as a hip, in-demand session cat. But he also saw the writing on the wall and graciously agreed to hire me as his assistant.

Each day, I opened the place at 9 a.m., fielded calls, and managed the interaction with the agency types and musicians. Eventually, I became proficient at composing on the Synclavier and wrote and produced dozens of jingles. I also went on Screen Actors Guild contracts as a singer and made a good living. I learned how to compose quickly and manipulate the digital data based on the direction I was given to make the clients happy.

I even got to hire some of the talented people I had previously worked with in my session days, including a couple of great bass players and celebrity artists like Dr. John. Quite ironic.

But after about five years, it became a bit of a paint-by-numbers exercise. At first, I felt like I was creating thirty-second pop songs for TV spots. But then I started wondering if there was something more interesting that I could do with my time *and still get paid for it.*

One day, a creative team from an advertising agency came into the studio and said bluntly, "We need a thirty-second 'Duran Duran-style' jingle for a new Clairol shampoo. And we need it by 9 a.m. tomorrow morning."

Now, I had just written a similar-style jingle for Dove Soap the week before, but I didn't say anything. I just went to work, and I stayed up most of the night writing and producing the track. It turned out fine, but after we handed the demos off and I had a chance to catch my breath, I realized I was done. The Jingle Biz had stopped being interesting or creative enough for me.

TEACHABLE MOMENT #8

Trust your own personal priorities when contemplating a career change. Go with your instincts. Don't ever be afraid to admit that you don't feel fulfilled in your current role and always be ready to move to your next one. And look for the next technology transformation for guidance! Your future self will thank you, believe me!

Transferring Existing Skills and Acquiring New Ones

An amazing new technology was just beginning to appear: the World Wide Web. Unlike many other people my age at the time, I was already pretty comfortable using a computer thanks to the advent of samplers, sequencers, and software programs for composing and arranging music. The Synclavier, for example, used a Mac as the main interface.

I found myself thinking: "Huh. Computers. Now maybe that's a place where I can use my creative and digital skills to make a living and do something new and interesting."

So, I began to explore.

This meant leaving the jingle house where I had been and going to work for another composer. Soon after, I proposed we build him one of those "newfangled website things" so he could be the first commercial music company in New York to have its own Internet presence. I told him we could post samples of his music to the site instead of having to send cassettes to producers and clients.

Much to my delight, he agreed!

I tracked down a graphic designer who knew how to code and prepare images for the Web. He had a friend who knew how to set up a Web server, and we were off. I spent a few months collecting content and managing these two guys to produce his website. I was hooked!

The key to this particular transition was realizing the clear similarities between the Jingle Biz and website production. Of course, there were different actors, but it seemed to me that in both cases, there was always a client, a budget, and a deliverable.

So, I figured out who the players were in the Web business, what skills each one had, and what their roles were in the overall production process. Then, I learned enough about each role to articulate what was needed and provide guidance about how it might get done. I did this by taking numerous classes, reading a lot of books, attending various computer user group meetings, and staying up late surfing the nascent Web, looking at source code to see how sites were put together.

I essentially transferred my "producing" skills to this new setting. It took hard work, but I was excited about this new opportunity, and I managed to make the shift, eventually offering my skills as a website producer full-time.

A headhunter found me somehow and got me a job at a seminal interactive agency in New York called CKS Partners. I worked there for about a year and then went to another agency called Eagle River Interactive, managing website production for various large companies like Johnson & Johnson and Sedgwick.

TEACHABLE MOMENT #9

You have skills that you have acquired growing up, in school, in the workforce, at camp, and in any number of settings—both formal and informal. Keep this in mind when making your career shifts. Figure out what to leverage and what you need to learn. And how and where to learn it.

Reality Bytes

It's hard to believe now, but back in the 1990s, nobody really knew if this Web thing would have any real global impact. Would it be a tool for social good? Could you maybe buy and/or sell stuff using it? Would people actually do business using it?

A random encounter on a commuter train led me to probably the most dramatic transition of my career path so far, taking me from the scrappy and ever-morphing land of rock 'n roll and music for television into a decade and a half inside the belly of a Global 50 multinational technology company. On some level, it's still hard for me to even believe it.

One Sunday morning, I happened to be commuting from Connecticut into midtown Manhattan. I sat down on the Metro-North train next to a young woman named Abigail who was working on her laptop. She and I started to chat, commiserating over the fact that we were both commuting into the city for work on a beautiful summer weekend.

Turns out, she was heading downtown to work on "Deep Blue," IBM's supercomputer that was using what we now can identify as an early form of artificial intelligence. We had a nice chat, exchanged email addresses, and agreed to keep in touch. About six months later, I got an email from her saying that her department was expanding and asking if I had any interest in possibly working at IBM.

I had a knee-jerk reaction.

"Wow, I don't think so—what would *I* do at IBM?"

It turns out, they were increasing their focus on the web and were looking to build a team of Account Managers for their Corporate Internet Programs division. They needed people who knew how to produce websites that could go into the various business units and help executives figure out how to use the new technology.

I initially balked, as it seemed like an unlikely fit. But Abigail encouraged me to interview with her VP anyway. She reminded me that, at the very least, I would have an interesting conversation. So, I reluctantly agreed to go to the meeting, fully expecting to be quickly escorted to the door by some admin wearing a smirk.

The interview was way downtown, basically right across from the New York Stock Exchange. I walked in, sat down and handed the VP my resume; it included all my myriad musical escapades over the years, and so I immediately launched into a disclaimer.

"You see, I was a touring rock musician for ten years and have been producing music for TV and radio for the past six years so, um, yeah."

In that moment, dear reader, I honestly thought she would throw me out of her office. But she studied my resume for a moment more, before looking up.

"I get it," she said at last. "I am a singer myself. The same qualities that made you successful as a freelance musician in New York will make you successful at IBM. You are going to need to be a creative problem solver here—resourceful and resilient—comfortable with ambiguity, able to work across disciplines, and aware of your role as a global citizen."

After a two-beat pause, she said, "Can you start next week?"

I nearly fell out of my chair.

I was dumbfounded. I couldn't believe that a company with the prestige and reputation of IBM would be interested in hiring me. Now to be candid, this was really just a case of being in the right place at the right time. While I'd like to think I was someone special, to be honest, it was a very simple case of supply and demand.

TEACHABLE MOMENT #10

Companies don't hire people based on looks or connections or hairstyle or even education these days. They hire people who can help them drive a business model to generate attributable revenue. It's just that simple. You have to make sure you are the "product" they want to "buy." You need to have the right skills for the career you are moving to.

Always remember that you are acquiring skills throughout your various careers that you can apply in various settings—valuable skills are needed in many disciplines to help drive business models.

Learning to Trust Your Gut

The woman who hired me at IBM was able to see the big picture. She realized that I had a set of meta-skills that could be transferred into a complex, matrixed corporate organization and that I also had the specific skill she needed. *I knew how to produce websites.* I soon discovered she had assembled a whole team of people with very different backgrounds. One woman was a former dancer turned film director. Another, a graphic design professor at NYU. One was a guitar player turned direct marketing exec. But what we all had in common was business experience, creativity, and basic understanding, not only of the tactics required to build a website but also of what the broader business implications might be. The Web is now, of course, deeply integrated into society and business. But back then, no one really knew what the heck was going to happen with it. I used to say to IBM clients, "Yeah, I've been involved in the Web since back when it was hip!"

In terms of everyday work, I found myself quickly moving from being a Web producer into a business strategy role. I worked with our account manager team to help executives at IBM use the Web to sell stuff, provide customer support, better manage business partner interactions, improve efficiency in the supply chain, and deal with journalists and analysts.

In 1999, at the height of the "dot-com bubble," the web was transforming how companies did business, and there were many opportunities. Several companies contacted me, but one called Proxicom approached me about coming to work for them. They were flush with cash after a recent IPO and were hiring frantically from all kinds of companies, such as big tech, consulting firms, and multimedia ad agencies.

They offered me a 40 percent bump in salary, a Director title, and a set of stock options. I figured I would strike while the proverbial iron was hot. I was not totally enamored with the people there, but it looked like a smart move on paper. So, I took their offer and left IBM.

My first day on the job, I realized I had made a huge mistake. The people were obnoxious. Pompous. Arrogant.

Unsympathetic. There was a clear but subtly manifest divide between the employees who had worked at the company before the IPO and the "gold-diggers" like me who had joined afterward, seemingly looking to cash in on the legacy employees' hard work.

I immediately hated the place and its culture, and I realized I had to leave.

As luck would have it, I had joined Proxicom in January of 2000, and by the middle of April, NASDAQ had gone south. The "dot-com bubble" had burst. By November, most of the company's high-flying Wall Street clients had gone away, and the office had metaphorical tumbleweeds. Around this time, my VP invited me to her office and announced that I was being fired and that I would need to pack up and leave immediately. I was so relieved that I could barely get out of there fast enough.

Fortunately, I had stayed in touch with a couple of people from the IBM team, and one of them asked if I would be interested in coming back. I said "Absolutely!"

I returned to IBM in November 2000 and worked there for another thirteen years. The good news from this story is that when I went back to IBM, I demanded they pay me at my new salary level. And they did.

TEACHABLE MOMENT #11

Yet another lesson I learned the hard way: trust your gut when looking for your next career. Do not let the facts on paper override your primal instincts. When I moved to Proxicom from IBM, I did not listen to my gut, and it led me to endure a nine-month ordeal working with a bunch of real jerks.

Rock 'N Roll in a Corporate Setting

After returning to IBM, I began to get the itch to be in a more public role, recasting my rock 'n roll persona in a corporate setting. Periodically, I saw executives present in front of large audiences and spout a series of numbers about sales targets, global growth numbers, margin increases, free cash flow, and productivity gains. And I thought, "You know, I could probably do that."

The good news for me was that there was an increasing demand for speakers who could tell the IBM On Demand Business story in front of clients, and not all execs were comfortable or available to do that. I asked if I could be trained, and my next adventure was soon underway.

Over the next several years, I presented to numerous IBM clients in various settings around the New York area. I loved it. I learned how to deliver a convincing pitch, think on my feet, and field relevant (and irrelevant) questions. I trained myself to think of these presentations as one-act plays, creating a story with a beginning, middle, and end. I got pretty good at it.

After a few years, I began to look for a more creative role perhaps in marketing or communications. I interviewed with the VP of Human Resources Communications at IBM Corporate Headquarters and the job description basically had three parts.

She decided that I had transferable skills that would enable me to run a large financial education project for employees. For the second piece, she would teach me how to create what she called a Manager's Package for communicating with the various business units. And the third piece she would delegate to another person on her team.

I worked there for a couple of years. My first role in Corporate Headquarters at a global tech business!

TEACHABLE MOMENT #12

*I had some skills applicable to this new role at Corporate Headquarters, but the hiring VP offered to teach me a **new** set of required skills. She also agreed to move part of the job to another person. End result? She got her needs met, and I got a new job. This happens more often than you think, dear reader, so keep this in mind when looking for a new role. If you have 60 percent of the required skills and you are attracted to the job, go for it!*

My final years at IBM were in Global Financing, where I worked in an executive communications role. Then, after fifteen years at the company, I realized I had learned and enjoyed as much as I could stand. During one of the company's ongoing "Resource Actions" (read: laying people off), I was offered a package. Since I was old enough and had enough years of service to retire, I took it.

Bye-bye, Big Blue. It was fun.

The Lightbulb Moment: Future of Work

By now, you may be asking, how did I become a workplace futurist? What was the catalyst?

Well, as I said earlier, in 2001, my alma mater, Bennington College, invited me to deliver a keynote address to kick off a series of Senior Week activities. They wanted me to describe how I had applied what I had learned at the college, the idea that you need to own your own learning and that your path will constantly evolve. They had asked me to deliver a presentation to inspire the graduating class.

I did some due diligence on the state of learning and working and realized that I was, in fact, the poster child for the way that today's learners will operate in the global borderless workplace of the twenty-first century. That they will have multiple careers, just like I have had. They will acquire, leverage, and unlearn a range of skills throughout their work lives. It hit me that I could possibly inspire these students to do great things and help them realize that there are lots of exciting opportunities ahead of them.

That kicked off my research, which involved analyzing and codifying how I had navigated my multiple careers. I also conducted a study on how the workplace has evolved and how careers are changing with it.

After leaving IBM in June of 2013, I connected with a company called Future Workplace, a boutique HR consulting firm based in New York. In fact, I found the woman who ran the company using a LinkedIn search. I spent a couple of years further consolidating my thinking around the skills and career opportunities that lie ahead. However, the clients of this company were HR executives, and it became clear to me that my passion is in enabling and empowering learners and workers.

Based on this, I developed a presentation and workshop called "How to Succeed at Jobs That Don't Exist Yet." I've presented it in various settings, from business schools to seventh-grade career days. With a friend, I developed a series of activities that I call my Future Career Toolkit, an actionable set of tools that will help today's learners be successful in the new workplace paradigm. That is the core content of this book.

In keeping with my curiosity about bleeding-edge tech and my passion for reinvention, I became fascinated by quantum information science about five years ago. I joined the Quantum Economic Development Consortium (QED-C), a Federally funded organization comprised of over 150 members, including leading quantum companies, prestigious academic institutions, and members of the National Laboratory network. As a member of the Workforce Technology Committee, I am helping develop strategies for empowering and enabling the quantum-ready workforce. It's exciting stuff!

Leveraging my showbiz background yet again, I've also acted as the Master of Ceremonies for many Quantum Technology events for sponsors like The Economist, Inside Quantum Technology, and Alpha Events. Over the past few years, I have been hired to be the Master of Ceremonies at tech events in Silicon Valley, Miami, Montreal, London, Paris, and Singapore.

I hosted the Quantum Tech Pod for three years. The podcast features interviews with C-suite executives at leading quantum companies who discuss how they got into this field and what they plan to do with this incredible technology.

I am now hosting Qubit Confidential, a video podcast series where I speak with thought leaders in the quantum space.

Oh . . . and I still play bass with a few different groups, including a New Orleans R&B band called Otis & The Hurricanes and another band hard-core Cajun dance band called River City Slim and the Zydeco Hogs. In the summer, I often do two to three gigs a month! Music is my "hobby deluxe" and personal therapy now.

And the exciting takeaway from my story? You, like me, have the potential to successfully navigate multiple careers, too!

IMAGES FROM THE JOURNEY

Playing with McKendree Spring about to open for The Eagles, 1973.

180 | Improvising Careers

My power trio at CBGBs, New York City, 1980.

On the set of the TV movie "Svengali" with Peter O'Toole, 1983.

Presenting the Virtual Green Data Center to the IBM Board of Directors, 2007.

Practitioner Residency at The Rockefeller Foundation's
Bellagio Center on Lake Como, Italy, 2011.

My talk at TEDxTimesSquare "Open Technologies for 430,000 Employees," 2013.

My Story | 183

Master of Ceremonies at The Economist's Business Innovation Summit, London, 2022.

Host of the Qubit Confidential podcast for Alpha Events, 2025.

ABOUT THE AUTHOR

Christopher Bishop is a nonlinear multimodal careerist—he has had eight so far. Right after graduating from college with a degree in German literature, he got a gig touring with a country-rock band McKendree Spring. When the band broke up three years later, he moved to New York City, where he became a sought-after session musician, touring and recording with Robert Palmer, Darius Brubeck, Chuck Berry, Bo Diddley, and Ronnie Spector among many others.

Chris then broke into the jingle business, writing music for radio and TV commercials. He sang and played bass on the first Kit Kat jingle, "Gimme A Break." Becoming bored with that role —"another Duran Duran jingle for another shampoo?"—he taught himself to be a World Wide Web producer. After working at several seminal interactive agencies, he was hired by IBM into Corporate Internet Programs. He spent fifteen years at Big Blue in various roles. Along the way, he did a TEDxTimesSquare talk and was awarded a month-long Practitioner Residency at the Rockefeller Foundation's Bellagio Center on Lake Como.

Based on his own atypical career path, Chris developed a workshop titled "How to succeed at jobs that don't exist yet," designed to enable today's learners to navigate the twenty-first-century's global borderless workplace successfully.

He has also developed a "minds-on" interactive Future Career Toolkit workshop with three specific activities—VOICE, ANTENNA and MESH. These tools help participants determine their own personal brand, identify where conversations are taking place in their identified area of passion and then connect with the thought leaders pushing the envelope in that domain.

Bishop has delivered Future Career lectures and workshops in the US at numerous universities, including Baruch, Bennington, Columbia, Duke, Georgetown, NYU Stern School of Business, Texas A&M, Union, and Queens College. He has also given lectures in the UK at the London School of Economics, London Business School, King's College London, Royal Holloway University, the Institute of Physics, and the National Physical Laboratory.

Recasting his rock and roll persona, Chris performs the role of Master of Ceremonies and panel moderator at numerous events for The Economist, including their "Commercialising quantum" conferences, their Business Innovation Summit events, and their Metaverse Summit. He has also been the emcee and led panels at numerous quantum technology conferences in London, Los Angeles, Miami, Montreal, New York, Paris, Singapore, and San Francisco.

Over the past three years, he has released seventy-six episodes of the Quantum Tech Pod, in which he interviews

C-suite executives at leading quantum companies. Most recently, Chris has been hosting Qubit Confidential, a series of video podcasts with quantum thought leaders.

Chris is also an active Quantum Economic Development Consortium (QED-C) member and plays a key role on the Workforce Technical Advisory Committee. He initiated and managed their Office Hours initiative, hosting a monthly Zoom session that connected students in quantum information science with mentors in the private sector and at national labs.

Chris still plays with several different bands in Connecticut, where he lives, including Otis & The Hurricanes and River City Slim and the Zydeco Hogs.

He is available for career and life design consulting, lectures, and workshops on the future of work, technology, and careers.

ENDNOTES

Introduction
1. Smith, Morgan, "Gen Z and millennials are leading 'the big quit' in 2023—why nearly 70 percent plan to leave their jobs," CNBC, 2023, https://www.cnbc.com/2023/01/18/70%-of-gen-z-and-millennials-are-considering-leaving-their-jobs-soon.html.

Chapter 2
2. LADDERS. Research: "Remote Work Now Accounts for Nearly 15 percent of All High Paying Jobs," 2021, https://www.theladders.com/press/research-remote-work-now-accounts-for-nearly-15-of-all-high-paying-job.
3. Anderson, M.T. "In Medieval Europe, A Pandemic Changed Work Forever. Can It Happen Again?" *The New York Times*, 2022, https://www.nytimes.com/2022/02/16/opinion/sunday/covid-plague-work-labor.html.
4. Cook, Ian. "Who Is Driving the Great Resignation?" *Harvard Business Review*, 2021, https://hbr.org/2021/09/who-is-driving-the-great-resignation.
5. Krugman, Paul. "Wonking Out: Is the Great Resignation a Great Rethink?" *The New York Times*, 2021 https://www.nytimes.com/2021/11/05/opinion/great-resignation-quit-job.html.
6. Mendoza, Angelo. "37 percent of Remote Workers Would Quit Over an RTO Policy, but Company Culture Events Could Keep Them Engaged," Indeed, 2024, https://www.indeed.com/career-advice/news/workers-quit-over-return-to-work-policy.
7. West, Ty. "Hiring in the Covid Era: 5 factors that can make or break your search," *The Business Journal*, 2021 https://www.bizjournals.com/bizjournals/news/2021/08/25/hiring-covid-19-era-job-search.html.
8. Hsu, Andrea. "As the Pandemic Recedes, Millions of Workers Are Saying 'I Quit'." NPR, 2021, https://www.npr.

org/2021/06/24/1007914455/as-the-pandemic-recedes-millions-of-workers-are-saying-i-quit.

9 Stropoli, Rebecca. "Are We Really More Productive Working From Home?" Chicago Booth Review, 2021, https://www.chicagobooth.edu/review/are-we-really-more-productive-working-home.

10 Medici, Andy. "Quite quitting may be more widespread than ever. And managers are not immune." *The Business Journals*, 2022 https://www.bizjournals.com/bizjournals/news/2022/09/08/quiet-quitting-burnout-manager-hiring-firing.html?utm_source=pocket_mylist.

Chapter 3

11 Rattner, Steven. "Fear Not the Coming of the Robots." *The New York Times*, 2014, https://www.nytimes.com/2014/06/22/opinion/sunday/steven-rattner-fear-not-the-coming-of-the-robots.html.

12 Andrews, Evan. "Who Were the Luddites?" History, 2023, https://www.history.com/news/who-were-the-luddites.

13 Online Etymology Dictionary. https://www.etymonline.com/word/work.

14 Rushkoff, Douglas, *Team Human. W.W. Norton & Company*, 2019, https://www.amazon.com/Team-Human-Douglas-Rushkoff/dp/039365169X.

15 Encyclopedia Britannica. Industrial Revolution. https://www.britannica.com/event/Industrial-Revolution.

16 Associated Press. "Farm Population Lowest Since 1850s." *The New York Times*, 1988, https://www.nytimes.com/1988/07/20/us/farm-population-lowest-since-1850-s.html.

17 Osborne, Michael. Frey, Carl Benedikt. "Automation and the future of work—understanding the numbers." Oxford Martin School, 2018, https://www.oxfordmartin.ox.ac.uk/blog/automation-and-the-future-of-work-understanding-the-numbers/.

18 Hagel, John. "Capabilities and Emotions." Edge Strategy and the Future of Work, 2020 https://www.johnhagel.com/capabilities-and-emotions/.

19 O' Reilly, Tim. "Why we'll never run out of jobs." O'Reilly Media, 2016 https://www.youtube.com/watch?v=K7ZFxPnL0Ww.

Chapter 4

20 Lancaster, John. "The Invention of Money." *The New Yorker*, 2019 https://www.newyorker.com/magazine/2019/08/05/the-invention-of-money.

21 Wikipedia. Abacus. https://en.wikipedia.org/wiki/Abacus#Mesopotamia.

22 Encyclopedia Britannica. Difference Engine. https://www.britannica.com/technology/Difference-Engine.

23 Encyclopedia Britannica. ENIAC. https://www.britannica.com/technology/ENIAC.

24 Gibney, Elizabeth. "Hello quantum world! Google publishes landmark quantum supremacy claim." Nature, 2019, https://www.nature.com/articles/d41586-019-03213-z.

25 Swayne, Matt. "China's Quantum Supercomputer Sets Quantum Supremacy." *Quantum Insider*, 2021, https://thequantuminsider.com/2021/06/30/chinas-superconducting-quantum-computer-sets-quantum-supremacy-milestone/.

26 Friedman, Thomas. "World Is Flatter than Ever, Author Says." NPR, 2007, https://www.npr.org/templates/story/story.php?storyId=12779679#:~:text=World%20Is%20%27Flatter%27%20than%20Ever%2C%20Author%20Says%20Two%20years,has%20been%20released%20in%20paperback.

27 The Business Research Company. "Uber Rides Unchallenged In the Top Spot of the Global Taxi and Limousine Market." GlobalNewsWire, 2020, https://www.globenewswire.com/news-release/2020/11/25/2133871/0/en/Uber-Rides-Unchallenged-In-The-Top-Spot-Of-The-Global-Taxi-And-Limousine-Market.html.

28 Suria, Asif. "Airbnb: Worth More Than Marriott, Hilton & Hyatt Combined." Seeking Alpha, 2021.

29 Malone, Thomas. *The Future of Work*. Harvard Business Review Press, 2004.

Chapter 5

30 Perez, Carlota. *Technological Revolutions and Financial Capital: The Dynamics of Bubbles and Golden Ages*. Edward Elgar Publishing, 2003.

31 Reading Times." Examining the Effect of the Automobile on Horseshoeing in a Pennsylvania Town." *American Farriers Journal*, 2017,

https://www.americanfarriers.com/articles/8921-examining-the-affect-of-the-automobile-on-horseshoeing-in-a-pennsylvania-town.

32 The Transcontinental Railroad. "Locomotives—It's All About Steam." Linda Hall Library, 2024, https://railroad.lindahall.org/essays/locomotives.html.

33 Jones, Andy. "A Brief History of Railroad Watches, and their role in modern timekeeping." Second Hand Horology, 2023, https://www.secondhandhorology.com/blogs/news/a-brief-history-of-railroad-watches-and-their-role-in-modern-timekeepi?srsltid=AfmBOoo0juSu0F3X-gFljweyHsT3GrfohvwjF47-9Ml0wATAWF-GfF3M2.

34 Colias, Mike. "Gas Engines, and the People Behind Them, Are Cast Aside for Electric Vehicles." *Wall Street Journal, 2021, https://www.wsj.com/articles/gas-engines-cast-aside-electric-vehicles-job-losses-detroit-11627046285.*

35 Colias, Mike. "Gas Engines, and the People Behind Them, Are Cast Aside for Electric Vehicles." *Wall Street Journal, 2021, https://www.wsj.com/articles/gas-engines-cast-aside-electric-vehicles-job-losses-detroit-11627046285.*

Chapter 6

36 Domb, Cyril. James Clerk Maxwell. Britannica, 2024, https://www.britannica.com/biography/James-Clerk-Maxwell.

37 Thomas Alva Edison." Famous Scientists." The Art of Genius. https://www.famousscientists.org/thomas-alva-edison/.

38 History.com Editors. Guglielmo Marconi. History, 2023, https://www.history.com/topics/inventions/guglielmo-marconi.

39 Coulstring, Mark. "iPhone History: from the original iPhone to iPhone 16." Seamgen, 2023, https://www.seamgen.com/blog/iphone-history-original-iphone-to-current-iphone.

40 Standage, Tom. "The Victorian Internet: The Remarkable Story of the Telegraph and the Nineteenth Century's On-Line Pioneers." Bloomsbury USA, 2014.

41 Pope, Nancy. "The Story of the Pony Express." *Smithsonian, National Postal Museum, Volume 1, Issue 2, 1992, https://postalmuseum.si.edu/research/articles-from-enroute/the-story-of-the-pony-express.html.*

42 The Model T. Ford, 2024, https://corporate.ford.com/articles/history/the-model-t.html.

43 Plumer, Brad. "The 2016 Noble Prize in Chemistry, explained in 500 words." Vox, 2016, https://www.vox.com/2016/10/5/13171850/2016-nobel-prize-chemistry.

44 Sanders, Robert. "Sprinkling of neural dust opens door to electroceuticals." UC Berkeley News, 2016 https://news.berkeley.edu/2016/08/03/sprinkling-of-neural-dust-opens-door-to-electroceuticals/.

45 Le Page, Michael. "What is CRISPR?" *NewScientist, 2016, https://www.newscientist.com/definition/what-is-crispr/#:~:text=CRISPR%20is%20a%20technology%20that,alter%20that%20piece%20of%20DNA.*

46 Wakabayashi, Daisuke. "Self-Driving Uber Car Kills Pedestrian in Arizona, Where Robots Roam." *The New York Times*, 2018, https://www.nytimes.com/2018/03/19/technology/uber-driverless-fatality.html.

47 Ridden, Paul. "MIT Media Lab knits an expressive wearable MIDI keyboard "New Atlas 2021, https://newatlas.com/music/mit-media-lab-knittedkeyboard-ii/.

48 MIT Media Lab. Tangible Media Group. biologic, 2016. https://tangible.media.mit.edu/project/biologic/.

49 Poupyrev, Ivan. "A smarter wardrobe with Jacquard by Google." Google Blog, 2019, https://atap.google.com/jacquard/.

50 Erickson, Mandy. "Virtual reality system helps surgeons, reassures patients." Stamford Medicine News Center, 2017, https://med.stanford.edu/news/all-news/2017/07/virtual-reality-system-helps-surgeons-reassures-patients.html.

51 Street, Francesca. "Inside the space hotel scheduled to open in 2025." CNNTravel, 2022, https://www.cnn.com/travel/article/space-hotel-orbital-assembly-scn/index.html.

52 *ArchiExpo Magazine.* "Voyager Station, the First Hotel in Space by 2027." 2023, https://emag.archiexpo.com/voyager-station-the-first-hotel-in-space-by-2027/.

Chapter 7

53 GoodReads, 2024, https://www.goodreads.com/quotes/8-talent-hits-a-target-no-one-else-can-hit-genius.

54 History of European Universities. Wikipedia, 2024, https://en.wikipedia.org/wiki/University#:~:text=The%20word%20

university%20is%20derived,Europe%20by%20Catholic%20Church%20monks.
55 Polymath. Wikipedia, 2024, https://en.wikipedia.org/wiki/Polymath.
56 Shen Kuo. Wikipedia, 2024, https://en.wikipedia.org/wiki/Shen_Kuo.
57 Carlos de Sigüenza Góngora. Wikipedia, 2024, https://en.wikipedia.org/wiki/Carlos_de_Sig%C3%BCenza_y_G%C3%B3ngora.
58 Hildegard of Bingen. Wikipedia, 2024, https://en.wikipedia.org/wiki/Hildegard_of_Bingen.
59 Scivias. Wikipedia, 2024, https://en.wikipedia.org/wiki/Scivias.
60 Leon Battista Alberti. Wikipedia, 2024, https://en.wikipedia.org/wiki/Leon_Battista_Alberti.
61 Baldassare Castiglione. Wikipedia, 2024, https://en.wikipedia.org/wiki/Baldassare_Castiglione.
62 The Book of the Courtier. Wikipedia, 2024, https://en.wikipedia.org/wiki/The_Book_of_the_Courtier.
63 Useem, Jerry. "At Work, Expertise Is Falling Out of Favor," *The Atlantic, 2019, https://www.theatlantic.com/magazine/archive/2019/07/future-of-work-expertise-navy/590647/.*
64 Friedman, Thomas. "How to Get a Job at Google." *The New York Times, 2017, https://www.nytimes.com/2014/02/23/opinion/sunday/friedman-how-to-get-a-job-at-google.html.*
65 Thomas A. Edison. Goodreads, 2024, https://www.goodreads.com/quotes/8287-i-have-not-failed-i-ve-just-found-10-000-ways-that.
66 Tartakovsky, Margarita. "The Link Between Creativity and Eccentricity." PsychCentral, 2011, https://psychcentral.com/blog/the-link-between-creativity-and-eccentricity#3.
67 Simonton, Dean Keith. "Creativity and Discovery as Blind Variation: Campbell's (1960) BVSR Model after the Half-Century Mark." *Sage Journals, 2011, https://journals.sagepub.com/doi/abs/10.1037/a0022912.*

Chapter 8
68 Dass, Ram. *Be Here Now. Harmony, 1978.*

Chapter 9

69 Ralph Waldo Emerson. GoodReads. 2024, https://www.goodreads.com/quotes/876-to-be-yourself-in-a-world-that-is-constantly-trying.

70 Prabhakar, Kavitha. "Foster Innovation, Ethical Tech With Diverse Teams." *CIO Journal, The Wall Street Journal, 2020,* https://deloitte.wsj.com/articles/foster-innovation-ethical-tech-with-diverse-teams-01578948366.

Chapter 10

71 Tiku, Nitasha. "Google's CEO, Eric Schmidt, Finds You Woefully Unprepared for the Impending Revolution." *New York Magazine,* 2010, https://nymag.com/intelligencer/2010/08/googles_ceo_eric_schmidt_finds.html.

72 Takeo. "Can You Guess How Much Data Is Generated Everyday?" Takeo, 2023, https://www.takeo.ai/can-you-guess-how-much-data-is-generated-every-day.

73 Allan, David G. "Ben Franklin's '13 Virtues' path to personal perfection." CNN Health, 2018, https://www.cnn.com/2018/03/01/health/13-virtues-wisdom-project/index.html.

74 Fortis, Savannah. "Island nation turns to metaverse to preserve its disappearing heritage." Cointelegraph, 2022, https://cointelegraph.com/news/island-nation-turns-to-metaverse-to-preserve-its-disappearing-heritage.

75 Young, Liz. "Amazon Looks to Sparrow to Carry its Robotics Ambitions." *The Wall Street Journal, 2022,* https://www.wsj.com/articles/amazon-looks-to-sparrow-to-carry-its-robotics-ambitions-11668797969.

76 Voloschuk, Chris. "Metal Recycler Continuum Raises $36M in Funding." *Recycling Today, 2022,* https://www.recyclingtoday.com/news/metal-recycler-continuum-raises-36-million-dollars-in-funding/.

77 Fletcher, Claire. "Moon to Mars Initiative Round Three Grants Announced." Space Australia, 2021, https://spaceaustralia.com/index.php/news/moon-mars-initiative-round-three-grants-announced.

78 O'Shea, Dan. "Polarisqb, Auransa tout progress using quantum, AI in breast cancer project." Inside Quantum Technology News, 2022, https://www.insidequantumtechnology.com/news-archive/polaris-

qb-auransa-tout-progress-using-quantum-ai-in-breast-cancer-project/.

Chapter 11

79 Jansen, Michael. "Chance discovery favours the prepared mind," *Chem 13 News Magazine. University of Waterloo, 2014, https://uwaterloo.ca/chem13-news-magazine/march-2014/feature/chance-discovery-favours-prepared-mind.*

80 Kahn, Ashley. Hall of Fame Essay. Rock & Roll Hall of Fame, 2006, https://www.rockhall.com/inductees/miles-davis.

81 Futterman, Steve. "Miles Davis: 15 Essential Albums." *Rolling Stone, 1991, https://www.rollingstone.com/music/music-lists/miles-davis-15-essential-albums-247620/birth-of-the-cool-247639/.*

82 Harvard Medical School. "Dawn of social networks: Ancestors may have formed ties with both kin and non-kin based on shared attributes." Science Daily, 2012, https://www.sciencedaily.com/releases/2012/01/120125132610.htm.

83 Tillman, Nola Taylor. "Albert Einstein: Before and After Relativity." Space.com, https://www.space.com/25729-albert-einstein-before-after-relativity.html.

Chapter 12

84 McNamara, Paul. "Jennings explains his Jeopardy loss to Watson." Network World, 2011. https://www.networkworld.com/article/2228549/jennings-explains-his-jeopardy-loss-to-watson.html#:~:text=And%20it%20was%20with%20his,left%20to%20do%20but%20laugh.

Afterword

85 Dalio, Ray. *Principles.* Simon & Schuster, 2017, https://www.amazon.com/Principles-Life-Work-Ray-Dalio/dp/1501124021.

A free ebook edition is available with the purchase of this book.

To claim your free ebook edition:

1. Visit MorganJamesBOGO.com
2. Sign your name CLEARLY in the space
3. Complete the form and submit a photo of the entire copyright page
4. You or your friend can download the ebook to your preferred device

Print & Digital Together Forever.

Snap a photo   Free ebook   Read anywhere

www.ingramcontent.com/pod-product-compliance
Lightning Source LLC
Jackson TN
JSHW020424140825
89344JS00008B/276